CHANGING TRADE PATTERNS
IN MANUFACTURED GOODS:
An Econometric Investigation

CONTRIBUTIONS
TO
ECONOMIC ANALYSIS

176

Honorary Editor:
J. TINBERGEN

Editors:
D. W. JORGENSON
J. WAELBROECK

NORTH-HOLLAND
AMSTERDAM · NEW YORK · OXFORD · TOKYO

CHANGING TRADE PATTERNS IN MANUFACTURED GOODS: An Econometric Investigation

Bela BALASSA

John Hopkins University
and
The World Bank
Washington, D.C. 20433
U.S.A.

and

Luc BAUWENS

Université d'Aix-Marseille II
Marseille
France

1988
NORTH-HOLLAND ·
AMSTERDAM · NEW YORK · OXFORD · TOKYO

© ELSEVIER SCIENCE PUBLISHERS B.V., 1988

ISBN: 0 444 70492 2

Publishers:
ELSEVIER SCIENCE PUBLISHERS B.V.
P.O. Box 1991
1000 BZ Amsterdam
The Netherlands

Sole distributors for the U.S.A. and Canada:
ELSEVIER SCIENCE PUBLISHING COMPANY, INC.
52 Vanderbilt Avenue
New York, N.Y. 10017
U.S.A.

LIBRARY OF CONGRESS
Library of Congress Cataloging-in-Publication Data

Balassa, Bela A.
    Changing trade patterns in manufactured goods : an econometric
investigation / Bela Balassa and Luc Bauwens.
        p.   cm. -- (Contributions to economic analysis ; 176)
    Bibliography: p.
    Includes index.
    ISBN 0-444-70492-2 (U.S.)
    1. International trade--Econometric models. 2. Commercial policy-
-Econometric models. 3. Commercial products--Econometric models.
I. Bauwens, Luc, 1952-   . II. Title. III. Series.
HF1379.B35 1988
382'.4567--dc19   88-21747
                                                              CIP

PRINTED IN THE NETHERLANDS

INTRODUCTION TO THE SERIES

This series consists of a number of hitherto unpublished studies, which are introduced by the editors in the belief that they represent fresh contributions to economic science.

The term 'economic analysis' as used in the title of the series has been adopted because it covers both the activities of the theoretical economist and the research worker.

Although the analytical methods used by the various contributors are not the same, they are nevertheless conditioned by the common origin of their studies, namely theoretical problems encountered in practical research. Since for this reason, business cycle research and national accounting, research work on behalf of economic policy, and problems of planning are the main sources of the subjects dealt with, they necessarily determine the manner of approach adopted by the authors. Their methods tend to be 'practical' in the sense of not being too far remote from application to actual economic conditions. In addition they are quantitative.

It is the hope of the editors that the publication of these studies will help to stimulate the exchange of scientific information and to reinforce international cooperation in the field of economics.

The Editors

PREFACE

This volume examines the changing pattern of trade in manufactured goods by the use of econometric techniques. It analyzes the determinants of inter-industry specialization (Part I), those of intra-industry specialization (Part II), and the combined determinants of the two (Part III).

The method of investigation employed is cross-section analysis of data for thirty-eight developed and developing countries, for each of which manufactured goods accounted for at least 18 percent of total exports and surpassed $300 million in 1979. The results may further be interpreted in terms of the changes that occur in the pattern of specialization in the process of economic development.

Part I tests the Heckscher-Ohlin theory by introducing simultaneously trade flows, factor intensities, and factor endowments in the analysis. The results may be interpreted in terms of the "stages approach" to comparative advantage, according to which a country's trade pattern changes in a predictable manner as it accumulates physical and human capital.

Part II analyzes the determinants of intra-industry trade, including country as well as industry characteristics affecting this trade. The results may be interpreted in terms of changes in the extent, and in the determinants, of intra-industry specialization as countries reach higher income levels in the process of economic development.

Part III combines the determinants of inter-industry and intra-industry specialization, with the addition of gravitational variables. The results may be interpreted as complementing the stages approach to comparative advantage by the changing pattern of intra-industry specialization in the process of economic development.

Parts of the research were published in professional journals, including the Economic Journal, European Economic Review, Oxford Economic Papers, Prévision et Analyse Economique, Review of Economics and Statistics, and Weltwirtschaftliches Archiv, and in collective volumes, International Trade and Exchange Rates in the late Eighties and Imperfect Competition and International Trade: The Policy Implications of Intra-Industry Trade. The publishers have kindly given permission to the use of published material.

Bela Balassa is Professor of Political Economy at the Johns Hopkins University and Consultant at the World Bank; Luc Bauwens is Associate professor at the Université d'Aix-Marseille II, and formerly Researcher at the World Bank. Balassa developed the original plan of the research and the conceptual framework of the investigation; Bauwens was responsible for the econometric estimation.

At an early stage of the investigation Roger Bowden was associated with the research. At various times, able research assistants included Linda Pacheco, Marcus Noland, and Shigeru Akiyama. Norma Campbell valiantly and uncomplainingly performed the arduous task of typing and re-typing.

The authors are greatly indebted to the World Bank, where the bulk of the research was undertaken in the framework of the research project "Changes in Comparative Advantage in Manufactured Goods." Luc Bauwens also acknowledges the financial support of the Interuniversity College in Management of Belgium. The authors alone are responsible for the contents of this volume, however, that should not be interpreted to reflect the views of the organizations they have been associated with.

TABLE OF CONTENTS

LIST OF TABLES

LIST OF FIGURES

Part I
THE DETERMINANTS OF INTER-INDUSTRY TRADE
IN MANUFACTURED GOODS

Chapter 1

CONCEPTUAL AND MEASUREMENT ISSUES

1.1 Testing the Heckscher-Ohlin Theory

In setting out to explain the pattern of international trade by reference
to inter-industry differences in factor intensities and intercountry
differences in factor endowments, the Heckscher-Ohlin theory posits the
existence of a well-defined relationship among trade flows, factor
intensities, and factor endowments.   In his Sources of International
Comparative Advantage: Theory and Evidence, Edward E. Leamer correctly
notes that "the way to measure the accuracy of the theory is to obtain
direct and independent measures of all three concepts ...." (1984, p. 49).

Rather than introducing all three elements in their empirical
investigations, a long list of researchers, including Baldwin (1971 and
1979), Branson (1973), Stern (1976), Branson and Monoyios (1977), Stern
and Maskus (1981), Maskus (1983), and Urata (1983), attempted to infer the
relative factor endowments of a single country vis-à-vis the rest of the
world from the factor intensity of its trade.   This procedure is open to
several objections.

There are obvious inadequacies in testing the Heckscher-Ohlin theory from
data of a single country.   This will be the case, in particular, if the
country is an "outlier."   In fact, apart from Stern (Germany) and Urata
(Japan), the country chosen in every case was the United States.   While
this choice might have been dictated by data availabilies and by the
desire to provide an explanation for the Leontief paradox, the United

States represents an extreme case among trading countries.

Moreover, as Leamer and Bowen (1981) first showed by means of a three-dimensional example, the inference made about factor endowments from a cross-section regression of trade flows on factor intensities may be incorrect. Subsequently, Aw (1983) proved in the framework of a multi-country and multi-industry model that inferences about relative factor endowments from cross-section results obtained for the trade of a particular country cannot be made, unless very stringent conditons are met.

An alternative approach, utilized by Leamer (1974), Bowen (1983), and again Leamer (1984), attempted to test the Heckscher-Ohlin theory by relating trade flows to factor endowments. However, as Bowen, as well as Leamer, have admitted, there is no necessary relationship between the coefficients estimated in regard to factor endowments and the factor intensity of trade. Correspondingly, this method will not provide an appropriate test for the Heckscher-Ohlin theory either.

Following an earlier paper (Balassa, 1979b), this study tests the Heckscher-Ohlin theory by simultaneously introducing trade flows, factor intensities, and factor endowments in an empirical investigation of the pattern of comparative advantage in manufactured goods in a multi-country model. It utilizes data on exports, imports, and net exports to test the hypothesis that countries relatively well-endowed with capital (labor) will export relatively capital-intensive (labor-intensive) commodities. [1]

The study makes use of a three-factor model (physical capital, human capital, and labor), with labor as the numeraire. Thus, factor intensities are expressed in terms of physical and human capital per worker while factor endowments are defined by relating the endowment of physical and human capital to the size of the labor force.

---

[1] For a generalized formulation of the relationship among the three variables, see Deardorff (1982).

The study covers altogether 38 countries, for each of which manufactured goods accounted for at least 18 percent of total exports and surpassed $300 million in 1979, one of the benchmark years for the estimates. The 38 country sample has been divided into two country groups: 20 developed countries with at least $2254 a year per capita incomes in 1973, and 18 developing countries with at most $2031 per capita incomes.

The relevant data are shown in Table 1.1. The table also provides code numbers for each country, which are used in the figures of the individual chapters. Furthermore, participation in integration projects (the European Common Market, the European Free Trade Association, and the Latin American Free Trade Association) and location in Western Europe are shown in the table.

Sections 1.2, 1.3, and 1.4 provide information on the definition of the trade variables, the estimation of factor intensity coefficients, and the estimation of factor endowments, respectively. Section 1.5 contains a short outline of Chapters 2 and 3 that make up the rest of Part I of the volume.

1.2 Defining the Trade Variables

As trade in natural resource intensive products depends to a considerable extent on the country's resource endowment, the study is limited to comparative advantage in manufactured goods. The original investigation (Balassa, 1979b) was confined to exports, on the grounds that the commodity pattern of imports is greatly influenced by the system of protection.

Following earlier work by Balassa (1965), a country's relative export performance in the individual product categories was taken as an indication of its 'revealed' comparative advantage in the original investigation. For this purpose, the ratio of country's share in the world exports of a particular commodity to its share in the world exports of all manufactured goods was calculated. For example, a ratio of 1.10 (0.90) means that the country's share in a particular product category is

Part I

Table 1.1

List of Developed and Developing Countries

Name	Code	Per capita income (US$)	Integration projects a/	European countries
Developed Countries				
Switzerland	@	6758	–	+
U.S.A.	&	6244	–	–
Sweden	9	6204	F	+
Denmark	8	5743	C	+
Germany	7	5622	C	+
Australia	6	5529	–	–
Canada	5	5526	–	–
Norway	4	4926	F	+
France	3	4837	C	+
Belgium–Luxembourg	2	4758	C	+
Netherlands	1	4531	C	+
Japan	0	3840	–	–
Finland	Z	3758	F	+
Austria	Y	3674	F	+
U.K	X	3302	C	+
Israel	W	3015	–	–
Italy	V	2584	C	+
Ireland	U	2254	C	+
Developing Countries				
Spain	T	2031	–	+
Singapore	S	1920	–	–
Greece	R	1887	–	+
Argentina	Q	1559	L	–
Hong Kong	P	1498	–	–
Portugal	O	1367	F	+
Yugoslavia	N	1032	–	+
Mexico	M	880	L	–
Brazil	L	778	L	–
Taiwan	K	659	–	–
Malaysia	J	635	–	–
Tunisia	I	506	–	–
Korea	H	392	–	–
Morocco	G	381	–	–
Turkey	F	291	–	–
Egypt	E	283	–	–
Thailand	D	269	–	–
Philippines	C	266	–	–
India	B	130	–	–
Pakistan	A	96	–	–

Note: The data refer to 1973 and have been expressed in U.S. dollars at
        the average exchange rate for that year.
a/   C = European Common Market (EEC); F = EFTA; L = LAFTA
Source: World Bank economic and social data bank.

10 percent higher (lower) than its share in all manufactured exports. [1]

In a subsequent investigation (Balassa, 1984), 'revealed' comparative advantage was defined analogously with regard to imports. In the latter case, the ratio of a country's share in the world imports of a particular product category to its share in the world imports of all manufactured products was calculated, and a low (high) ratio was taken as an indication of a country's comparative advantage (disadvantage).

The errors involved in measuring 'revealed' comparative advantage in regard to exports and imports may be reduced by taking the difference between the two. Correspondingly, use was made of net exports (Balassa 1986, 1987), in addition to the export and import measures.

Net exports is the appropriate variable for gauging comparative advantage from the theoretical point of view in a free trade situation (Deardorff, 1982). At the same time, just like exports and imports, the net exports of individual countries in particular commodity categories had to be normalized in order to avoid size effects. Normalization has been done by expressing the net exports of country j in industry i $(X_{ij} - M_{ij})$ as a ratio of the sum of country j's exports and imports in industry i $(X_{ij} + M_{ij})$. [2] This ratio takes values between -1 and 1.

1.3 Estimating the Factor Intensity Coefficients

In the earlier investigation (Balassa, 1979b), use was made of U.S. data on capital coefficients for the years 1970 and 1971. This will be appropriate if factor substitution elasticities are zero. While this

---

[1] An alternative measure would involve relating exports to output in each country. In the absence of output figures, however, this measure could not be utilised in the present study. At any rate, it would require adjusting for country size while the measure used here makes such an adjustment.

[2] Lack of data for the individual countries did not permit scaling by the value of shipment as done by Branson and Monoyios (1977) in their investigation of the determinants of the U.S. trade pattern. On the importance of scaling, see Stern and Maskus (1981), p. 211.

assumption is not fulfilled in practice, Lary has shown variations in capital-intensity to be small in U.S.-U.K., U.S.-Japan, and U.S.-India comparisons as regards his value added measure (1968, Appendix D) although some recent estimates show larger divergences (Noland, 1988).

In a subsequent investigation (Balassa, 1984), Japanese coefficients for the year 1973 were utilized. Since Japan was in the middle of the scale in terms of relative capital endowments at that time, this procedure may permit limiting the error possibilities associated with the use of fixed input coefficients.

In the present study, estimates obtained with both American and Japanese coefficients are reported. This permits indicating the robustness of the results. It is also a substitute, however imperfect, for the use of variable coefficients.

In using American data, the U.S. Standard International Classification (SIC) has been used as the point of departure to define the manufacturing sector. From this category (SIC 19 to 39), we have excluded foods and beverages (SIC 20) and tobacco (SIC 21), where the high cost of transportation and the perishability of the basic material give an advantage to primary-producing countries. We have further excluded primary non-ferrous metals (SIC 333), as well as four-digit SIC categories covering textile waste, preserved wood, saw mill products, prefabricated wood, veneer and plywood, wood pulp, dyeing and tanning extracts, fertilizers, adhesives and gelatin, carbon black, petroleum refining and products, asbestos and asphalt products, cement and concrete, lime gypsum products, cut stone products, and lapidary work, the fabrication of which is greatly influenced by the domestic availability of the basic material. Also, ordnance (SIC 19), for which comparable trade data are not available, has excluded.

The product classification scheme used in this study has been established on the basis of the 4-digit SIC categories. Particular 4-digit categories have been merged in cases when the economic characteristics of the products in question were judged to be very similar and when comparable data did not exist according to the UN Standard International Trade

Classification, which has been used to collect trade figures. Altogether
167 product categories have been chosen (Table 1.2).

Data on the capital stock, employment, value added, and wages originate
from the U.S. Census of Manufacturing. In turn, the data for unskilled
wages have been taken from the Monthly Labor Review, published by the U.S.
Bureau of Labor Statistics; they relate to 2-digit industries, thus
involving the assumption that unskilled wages are equalised at this level.

In order to reduce the effects of variations due to the business cycle and
nonrecurring events, we have calculated simple averages of data for the
two years (1970 and 1971) under consideration. Finally, we have estimated
the value of human capital under the stock measure by discounting
differences between the average wage and the unskilled wage for the
individual product categories at a rate of 10 percent. [1]

Japanese data on capital stock, employment, value added, and wages
originate from the Census of Mining and Manufacturing Industry of Japan
for 1973. The Census data have been reclassified according to the U.N.
International Standard Industrial Classification (ISIC) scheme. Excluding
natural resource products, [2] altogether 97 five-digit ISIC categories
have been distinguished (Table 1.3). [3] The corresponding trade data have
been generated from the GATT tapes, utilizing the correspondence
established between the ISIC and the five-digit U.S. Standard

---

[1] This is in-between the discount rates of 9.0 and 12.7 percent used by
     Kenen (1965); the same discount rate was used by Fels (1972) and by
     Branson (1973).

[2] The excluded natural resource products with their ISIC numbers in
     parenthesis, are: Food products (311-2), Beverages (313), Tobacco
     (314), Textile waste (32191), Fur dressing and dyeing (3232), Lumber
     and its product (3311), Dyeing and tanning materials (35113), Chemical
     by-products (35114), Fertilizer and pesticides (3512), Petroleum
     refineries (3530), Miscellaneous products of petroleum and coal
     (3540), Cement, lime, and plaster (3692), and Miscellaneous mineral
     products (3699).

[3] The data have been generated by Anne Richards Loup for her Ph.D.
     dissertation successfully defended at the George Washington University
     in 1983.

Table 1.2

U.S. Industrial Classification Scheme Employed in the Calculations,

with the Standard International Trade Classification

Sector	Product Category	SIC	SITC
001	Cotton Fabrics (Grey)	2211	652.1
002	Synthetic Fabrics	2221,2262	653 (less 653.2, .3, .4, .9)
003	Woolen Fabrics	2231	653.2
004	Narrow Fabrics	2241	655.5, 655.9
005	Hosiery & Knit Fabrics	2251, 2252, 2256, 2259	841.4 (less 841.43, .44)
006	Knit Outwear	2253	841.44
007	Knit Underwear	2254	841.43
008	Cotton Fabrics (Finished)	2261	652.2
009	Woven Carpets & Rugs	2271	657.5
010	Nonwoven Carpets & Rugs	2272, 2279	657.6, 657.8
011	Yarn & Thread, Except Wool	2281,2282, 2284	651 (less 651.2, .5, .8, .9)
012	Woollen Yarn & Thread	2283	651.2
013	Felt Goods	2291	655.1
014	Lace & Embroidery	2292, 2395, 2396, 2397	654
015	Textile Paddings	2293	655.8
016	Nonrubberized Coated Fabrics	2295	611.2, 655.4
017	Cordage & Twine	2298	655.6
018	Textile goods nes	2299	651.5, 651.9, 653.3, 653.4, 653.9

New Sector	Product Category	SIC	SITC
019	Mens and Boys Outer Apparel	231, 2321, 2327, 2328, 2329	841.11
020	Nonknit Underwear	2322, 2341	841.1 (less 841.11, .12)
021	Ties, Corsets & Gloves	2323, 2342, 2381, 2389	841.2
022	Womens and Childrens Clothing	2331, 2335, 2337, 2339, 2361, 2363, 2369	841.12
023	Hats & Caps	2351, 2353	655.7, 841.5
024	Fur Goods	2371	842
025	Leather Clothing	2386, 3151	841.3
026	Curtains & Draperies	2391, 2392	656.6, 656.9, 657.7
027	Textile Bags & Sacks	2393	656.1
028	Canvas Products	2394	656.2
029	Wooden Boxes & Crates	2441, 2442, 2443	632.1
030	Cooperage Products	2445	632.2
031	Wood Products nes	2499	631.42, 632.7, 632.8, 633
032	Furniture & Fixtures	25	821, 895.1
033	Paper, Except for Construction	2621	641 (less 641.5, .6)
034	Paperboard	2631, 2641	641.5
035	Stationery	2642, 2645, 2649, 2761, 2782	642.2, 642.3

New Sector	Product Category	SIC	SITC
036	Paper Bags & Containers	2643, 2651, 2652, 2653, 2654	642.1
037	Paper Products nes	2646, 2647, 2655	642.9
038	Building Paper & Paper Products	2661	641.6
039	Newspapers & Periodicals	2711, 2721	892.2
040	Books	2731, 2732	892.1, 892.3
041	Miscellaneous Publishing	2741, 2751, 2752, 2771	892.4, 892.9
042	Engineering & Printing	2753, 3555	718.2
043	Inorganic Chemicals	2812, 2813, 2816, 2819	513 (less 513.27), 514, 515, 533.1, 561.1
044	Organic Chemicals	2815, 2818	512, 521, 531, 532.3, 551.2
045	Plastic Materials & Products	2821, 3079	581, 893
046	Synthetic Rubber	2822	231.2
047	Cellulosic Manmade Fibers	2823	266.3
048	Synthetic Fibers	2824	266.21, 266.22
049	Biological & Medicinal Products	2831, 2833, 2834	541 (less 541.9)
050	Soap & Cleansers	2841, 2842, 2843	554
051	Toilet Preparations	2844	553
052	Paints	2851	533.3
053	Misc. Agricultural Chemicals	2879	599.2
054	Explosives	2892	571.1, 571.2, 571.4
055	Printing Ink	2893	533.2

New Sector	Product Category	SIC	SITC
056	Misc. Chemical Preparations	2899	551.1, 571.3, 599.7, 599.9
057	Tires & Tubes	3011	629.1
058	Footwear	3021, 3141, 3142	851
059	Reclaimed Rubber	3031	231.3, 231.4
060	Misc. Rubber Products	3069	621, 629 (less 629.1), 841.6
061	Leather	3111	611 (less 611.2), 612
062	Industrial Leather Belting	3121	612.1
063	Leather Uppers	3131	612.3
064	Leather Bags & Purses	3161, 3171, 3172	831
065	Misc. Leather Goods	3199	612.2, 612.9
066	Flat Glass	3211	664.2, 664.4, 664.5
067	Glass Containers	3221, 3229, 3231	651.8, 664 (less 664.3, .4, .5), 665
068	Brick & Structural Clay Tiles	3251, 3253, 3259	662.4
069	Refractories	3255, 3297	662.3, 663.7
070	Vitreous Plumbing Fixtures	3261	812.2
071	Vitreous China Food Utensils	3262	666.4
072	Earthenware Food Utensils	3263	666.5
073	Porcelain Products	3264, 3269	663.9, 666.6, 723.2
074	Concrete & Brick Products	3271, 3272	663.6
075	Abrasive Products	3291	663.1, 663.2, 697.9
076	Asbestos Products	3292, 3293	663.8
077	Mineral Wool	3296	663.5

New Sector	Product Category	SIC	SITC
078	Misc. Nonmetallic Mineral Products	3299	663.4
079	Steel & Steel Products	3312, 3313, 3315, 3316, 3317, 3481, 3493, 3566	67 (less 671.3, 678.1, 678.5, 679) 693.2, 693.3, 694.1, 698.3, 698.6, 719.93
080	Iron Foundries	3321, 3322, 3494, 3497	678.1, 678.5, 679.1, 719.92
081	Steel Foundries	3323	679.2
082	Wrought Copper	3351	682.2
083	Wrought Aluminum	3352	684.2
084	Nonferrous Metals nes	3356, 3357	681, 683.2, 685.2, 686.2, 687.2, 688, 689 (less 689.31), 693.1, 723.1
085	Aluminum Castings & Stampings	3361, 3461	697.2
086	Brass, Bronze & Copper Castings	3362, 3369, 3392	698.8, 698.9
087	Iron & Steel Forgings	3391	679.3, 698.4
088	Primary Metal Products nes	3399	671.3
089	Metal Containers	3411, 3491, 3496	692.2
090	Cutlery	3421	696
091	Hand & Edge Tools	3423	695.1, 695.22, 695.23
092	Handsaws & Sawblades	3425	695.21
093	Hardware nes	3429	698.1
094	Sanitary & Plumbing Fixtures	3431, 3432	812.3
095	Nonelectric Heating Equipment	3433	719.13, 812.1
096	Structural Metal Products	3441, 3442, 3444, 3446, 3449	691, 693.4
097	Platework and Boilers	3443	692.1, 692.3 711.1, 711.2, 711.7
098	Bolts & Nuts	3452	694.2
099	Safes & Vaults	3492	698.2

New Sector	Product Category	SIC	SITC
100	Fabricated Metal Products nes	3499	719.66, 729.91
101	Steam Engines & Turbines	3511	711.3, 711.6, 711.8
102	Internal Combustion Engines	3519, 3714	711.5
103	Farm Machinery	3522	712, 719.64
104	Construction & Drilling Machinery	3531, 3532, 3533, 3544, 3545	695.24, 695.25, 695.26, 718.4, 718.51, 719.91, 719.54
105	Conveying & Carrying Equipment	3534, 3535, 3536	719.31
106	Industrial Trucks & Tractors	3537	719.32
107	Machine Tools	3541, 3542	715.1
108	Metal and Woodworking Machinery	3548, 3553	715.22, 715.23, 719.52, 719.53, 729.6
109	Food Products Machinery	3551	718.3, 719.62
110	Textile & Laundry Machinery	3552, 3582, 3633	717.1 (less 717.14), 725.02
111	Paper Making Machinery	3554	718.1
112	Special Industry Machines nes	3559	715.21, 717.14, 717.2, 718.52, 719.19, 719.51, 719.61, 719.8
113	Air Compressors & Pumps	3561, 3564, 3586	719.21, 719.22
114	Ball & Roller Bearings	3562	719.7
115	Industrial Furnaces & Ovens	3567, 3623	719.14, 729.92
116	General Industrial Machinery nes	3569	719.11, 719.23
117	Typewriters	3572	714.1
118	Computers	3573	714.3
119	Calculating & Accounting Machines	3574	714.2
120	Scales & Balances	3576	719.63
121	Office Machinery nes	3579	714.9

New Sector	Product Category	SIC	SITC
122	Automatic Merchandising Machines	3581	719.65
123	Refrigeration Machinery	3585	719.12, 719.15
124	Nonelectrical Machinery nes	3599	719.94, 719.99
125	Electric Meauring Instruments	3611	729.5, 729.99
126	Transformers, Motors & Generators	3612, 3621	722.1
127	Carbon & Graphite Products	3624	729.96
128	Household Cooking Equipment	3631	697.1
129	Household Refrigerators & Freezers	3632, 3639	719.4, 725.01
130	Electrical Housewares & Fans	3634, 3635	725 (less 725.01, .02)
131	Sewing Machines	3636	717.3
132	Electric Lamps	3641	729.2, 729.42
133	Lighting Fixtures	3642	729.94, 812.4
134	Radio & TV Equipment	3651, 3662	724 (less 724.91), 729.7, 729.93, 891.1
135	Phonographic Records	3652	891.2
136	Telephone & Telegraph Apparatus	3661	724.91
137	Electronic Components & Accessories	3671, 3672, 3673, 3674, 3679	722.2, 729.3, 729.95, 729.98
138	Storage Batteries	3691	729.12
139	Primary Batteries	3692	729.11
140	X-Ray Apparatus & Tubes	3693	726
141	Automotive Electrical Equipment	3694	729.41
142	Motor Vehicles & Bodies	3711, 3712, 3713	732 (less 732.9)
143	Trailers	3715, 3791, 3799	733.3
144	Aircraft	3721	734 (less 734.92)

New Sector	Product Category	SIC	SITC
145	Aircraft Engines & Equipment	3722, 3723, 3729	711.4, 734.92
146	Ships & Boats	3731, 3732	735
147	Locomotives and Parts	3741	731.1, 731.2, 731.3
148	Railroad Cars	3742	731 (less 731.1, .2, .3)
149	Motorcycles, Bicycles & Parts	3751	732.9, 733.1
150	Scientific Instruments & Control Equipment	3811, 3821, 3822	861.8, 861.9 (less 861.92, .94)
151	Optical Instruments	3831	861.1, 861.3
152	Medical Appliances & Equipment	3841, 3842, 3843	541.9, 733.4, 861.7, 899.6
153	Opthalmic Goods	3851	861.2
154	Photographic Equipment & Supplies	3861	861.4, 861.5, 861.6, 862
155	Watches & Clocks	3871	864
156	Jewelry & Silverware	3911, 3912, 3914	897.1
157	Musical Instruments & Parts	3931	891 (less 891.1, .2)
158	Games & Toys	3941, 3942	894.2
159	Childrens Vehicles	3943	894.1
160	Misc. Sporting Goods	3949	894.3, 894.4
161	Writing Instruments & Materials	3951, 3952, 3953, 3955	895 (less 895.1)
162	Costume Jewelry	3961	897.2
163	Buttons	3963	899.5
164	Needles, Pins & Fasteners	3964	698.5
165	Brooms & Brushes	3991	899.2
166	Hard Floor Coverings	3996	675.4
167	Miscellaneous Manufactures nes	3999	613, 861.92, 861.94, 894.5, 899 (less 899.2, .5, .6)

Annex to Table 1.2

(1) <u>Identification of all cases where 5-digit SITC codes are missing</u>. The
    rule is: if a country reports external trade in a 4-digit SITC item
    and there are <u>valid</u> 5-digit SITC codes or 5-digit SITC <u>UN special</u>
    codes corresponding to that 4-digit item then it is assumed that the
    5-digit data exists but is not reported at the required lowest level
    of disaggregation.

(2) <u>Calculation of total world trade corresponding to those 4-digit and
    missing 5-digit SITC groups identified in (1)</u>. If a country reports
    <u>imports</u> of a 4-digit commodity item then in order to calculate
    estimates of the missing 5-digit SITC subgroups the world's <u>exports</u> in
    the corresponding 4- and 5-digit codes are calculated, and vice versa
    for a country's exports.

(3) <u>Estimation of missing (unreported) 5-digit SITC items</u>. The
    methodology used in the estimation can be performed only for those
    reporter countries for which partial trade data (i.e., 4-digit level)
    exists in the World Bank Data Base.

- For a given country the reported trade in imports (exports) of a 4-
  digit SITC item or 5-digit SITC UN special code item is matched with
  total world exports (imports) corresponding to that item.

- The total world trade breakdown into 5-digit categories is used to
  establish a given country's trade structure.

- Finally, the weights calculated from world imports from the country
  concerned are applied to its 5-digit SITC export figure.

Table 1.3

Japanese Industrial Classification Scheme Employed
in the Calculations, and Correspondence with
Standard Industrial Trade Classification Schemes

Sector	Product Category	ISIC	SITC
01	Cotton fabrics, woven, grey	32111	652
02	Woven woolen fabrics	32112	6532
03	Woven fabrics of synthetic or artificial fiber	32113	6535 + 6536
04	Textile fabrics, woven, other than cotton, wool or synthetic	32114	6531 + 6533 + 6534 + 6538 + 6539
05	Tulle, lace, ribbons, trimmings & other small accessories	32115	654 - 65406
06	Textile yarn & thread	32116	651 - 65194
07	Fiber & wool prepared for textile use	32117	2216 + 261 - 2611 + 2622
08	Special textile fabrics & related products	32118	6555 + 65691 + 6577 + 6578
09	Embroidery	32121	65406
10	Textile bags & sacks & canvas products	32122	65583 + 6561 + 6562
11	Articles of misc. fabrics, cut or sewn	32123	26702 + 6566 + 65691 + 65692 + 6577 + 84144 + 899958
12	Knitting mills	3213	2629 + 26702 + 6537 + 84142 + 84145
13	Carpets, carpeting & rugs, knotted	32141	6575
14	Other carpets, carpeting & rugs & floor mats	32142	26702 + 6551 + 6576 + 6578
15	Cordage rope & twine industries	3215	2652 + 26702 + 165194 + 6556
16	Manufactures of textiles, n.e.s.	32192	6551 + 6554 - 65545 + 6558 - 65583 + 6559 + 65692 + 6574
17	Men's & boys' outerwear (not knitted or crocheted)	32201	84111
18	Women's girls' and infants' outerwear	32202	84112
19	Underwear & clothing accessories of textile fabric	32203	84113 + 84114 + 8412
20	Wearing apparel & clothing accessories of leather (excl. gloves)	32204	8413 + 842
21	Headgear	32205	6557 + 8415 - 84159
22	Wearing apparel & accessories, knitted or crocheted	32206	2118 + 84141 + 84143 + 84144 + 8416
23	Tanneries and leather finishing	3231	611
24	Synthetic rubber & rubber substitutes	35131	2312
25	Manufacture of products of leather & leather substitute excl. footwear	3233	612 - 6123 + 831 + 89991
26	Manufacture of footwear, excl. vulcanized or non-rubber or plastic	3240	6123 + 85 - 85101

27	Wooden & cane containers	3312	6321 + 6322 + 6578 + 89921 + 89922
28	Wood & cork products, n.e.s.	3319	244 − 24401 + 6327 + 6328 + 633 + 86193
29	Furniture & fixtures, except primarily of metal	3320	7173 + 72499 + 821 − 82102 − 82109
30	Newsprint & other printing & writing paper, paper & paperboard in rolls or sheets	34112	641 − 64194 − 64195 − 64196 − 64197 + 64293
31	Containers & boxes of paper & paperboard	3412	2511 + 6421 + 64294
32	Pulp, paper & paperboard articles, n.e.s.	3419	2511 + 64196 + 64197 + 6422 + 64291 + 64299
33	Paper & paperboard in rolls or sheets, exercise books, etc.	34201	2511 + 64194 + 64195 + 6423
34	Books & pamphlets, newspapers, periodicals, postcards, etc.	34202	71822 + 892 − 89292 + 89424 + 89425
35	Organic chemicals	35111	512 − 51226
36	Inorganic & radioactive materials	35112	51 − 512 − 51327 − 51328
37	Synthetic & artificial fibers suitable for spinning	35132	2662 − 26623 + 2663 − 26633 + 58131
38	Products of condensation & polycondensation	35133	58 − 58131
39	Paints, varnishes & lacquers	3521	5333 − 53331 − 53332 − 53333 + 59995
40	Drugs & medicines	3522	541 − 5419 + 54199 + 59977
41	Soaps & cleaning preparations, perfumes, cosmetics	3523	51226 + 55 − 551
42	Chemical products, n.e.s.	3529	29291 + 43142 + 43143 + 51327 + 5332 + 53332 + 53333 + 551 − 55123
43	Tire & tube industries	3551	6291
44	Manufacture of rubber products, n.e.s.	3559	2313 + 2314 + 62 − 62103 − 6291 + 65545 + 72322 + 84159
45	Manufacture of plastic products, n.e.s.	3560'	72322 + 72499 + 84159 + 85101 + 893 − 89422 + 89423 + 89921
46	Manufacture of pottery, china & earthenware	3610	27699 + 66244 + 66245 6639 + 666 + 72321 + 72322 + 8122
47	Manufacture of glass & glass products	3620	664 + 665 + 72322 + 81241 + 89425
48	Manufacture of structural clay products	3691	6623 + 6624 − 66244 − 66245 + 6637
49	Iron & steel basic industries	3710	27661 + 56121 + 67 + 69311 + 6932 + 71521 + 71991 + 7317
50	Wrought copper	37201	6822
51	Wrought aluminum	37202	6842
52	Cutlery	38111	696 − 69606
53	Hand tools & general hardware	38112	695 − 69526 + 6981 + 6984 + 69853 + 7122 + 71941 + 72992
54	Tubes, pipes & structural parts, tanks, vats, etc. (excl. plastic)	38131	691 + 6921 + 6923 + 71521 + 71966
55	Boilers	38132	7111 + 7112 + 7117
56	Nails, bolts, nuts	38191	694
57	Metal containers of iron, steel, aluminum used for transport of goods & misc. metal products	38192	6922 + 6933 + 6934 + 6971 − 69711 + 6972 − 69721 + 69792
58	Engines & turbines	3821	7113 − 71132 + 7115 + 7116 + 7118
59	Agricultural machinery & equipment	3822	712 − 7122 − 71231 − 7125
60	Metal & wood working machinery	3823	59526 + 715 − 71521 + 71952 + 71954 + 71991 + 7296 + 86193
61	Construction & mining machinery	38241	7125 + 7184 + 71951

No.	Description	Code	Composition
62	Other special machinery equipment	38242	71231 + 717 - 7173 + 718 - 01822 - 7184 + 71914 + 71962
63	Typewriters, calculating & statistical machinery duplication machinery	38251	7141 + 7149 + 71963
64	Computers	38252	7142 + 7143
65	Lifting & loading machinery	38291	7193 + 7324
66	Sewing machines	38292	7173
67	General industrial machinery	38293	5714 + 69711 + 71521 + 7191 - 71914 + 7192 - 71921 + 71942
68	Electrical industrial machines & apparatus	3831	7221 + 7222 + 72941 + 72991 + 72992 + 72995
69	Radio & television components	38321	7222 + 7241 + 7242 + 72492
70	Telephone & telegraph equipment	38322	72491 + 72499
71	Gramophone records & recorded tape	38323	8912
72	Misc. electronic components	38324	7261 + 7262 + 7293 + 72993 + 72994 + 8911
73	Electrical appliances & housewares	3833	72503 + 72504 + 72505
74	Batteries & accumulators	38391	7291
75	Electric lamps	38392	7261 + 7292 + 72942
76	Misc. electrical apparatus & supplies	38393	7222 + 7231 + 72322 + 72323 + 72992 + 72996 + 72998 + 72999
77	Shipbuilding & repairing	3841	71132 + 7115 + 735 - 7358
78	Manufacture of railroad equipment	3842	71132 + 731 - 73163 - 7317
79	Road motor vehicles	38431	7115 + 71921 + 73163 + 732 - 7324 - 7329
80	Trailers	3843	7333
81	Motorcycles & bicycles	3844	7115 + 7329 + 7331 + 7334 + 89421
82	Aircraft	3845	7114 + 734
83	Transport equipment n.e.s.	5849	8941
84	Medical equipment & supplies	38511	5419 - 54199 + 59991 + 71914 + 82102 + 8617 + 8996
85	Measuring & controlling equipment, other professional equipment	38512	7295 + 7297 + 8618 + 8619 + 86191 - 86193 - 86196 + 89927
86	Ophthalmic goods	38521	8611 + 8612
87	Optical instruments	38522	8613 + 86191 + 86193 + 86196
88	Photographic & cinematographic equipment	38523	8614 + 8615 + 8616
89	Manufacture of watches & clocks	3853	864 - 86429
90	Jewelry & related articles	3901	28502 + 6672 + 6673 + 6674 + 69606 + 69721 + 86429 + 8971
91	Musical instruments	3902	8914 + 8918 + 8919
92	Sporting & athletic goods	3903	8944 + 89991
93	Needles, pins, fasteners	39091	69852 + 7173
94	Toys, ornaments	39092	59991 + 89423 + 89424 + 89425 + 8972 + 8991 + 89922
95	Writing & copying supplies	39093	64195 + 64292 + 8952 + 89593 + 89594
96	Brooms & brushes	39094	8992 - 89921 - 89922 - 89927
97	Pipies, lighters, & related items, umbrellas	39095	29197 - 53333 - 89934 89935 + 8994 + 8995 - 89954 + 8999

International Trade Classification (SITC).

Data for unskilled wages derive from the publication of the Japanese
Ministry of Labor, <u>1973 Industrial Wage Structure</u>. [1] As in the previous
case, the value of human capital under the stock measure has been
estimated by discounting differences between the average wage and the
unskilled wage for individual product categories at a rate of 10 percent.

Capital intensity may be defined in terms of stocks (the value of the
capital stock plus the discounted value of the difference between average
wages and the unskilled age, divided by the number of workers or flows (a
variant of Lary's measure of value added per worker). The former approach
was used by Kenen (1965) and subsequently by Fels (1972) and by Branson
(1973).

The stock measure of capital intensity (k^s) is expressed in (1.1)

$$k_i^s = p_i^s + h_i^s = p_i^s + \frac{\bar{w}_i - w_i^u}{r^h} \tag{1.1}$$

for industry i, where p_i and h_i respectively, refer to physical and
human capital per man, $\bar{w}_i$ is the average wage rate, w_i^u the wage of
unskilled labor, and r^h the discount rate used in calculating the stock
of human capital. This approach implicitly assumes that the rental price
of physical capital, i.e. the risk-free rate of return and the rate of
depreciation, is the same in all industries. This assumption is made
explicit in expressing the flow equivalent (FE) of the stock measure of
capial intensity as in (1.2), where r^p is the

$$\text{(FE) } k_i^s = p_i^s (r^p + d) + (\bar{w}_i - w_i^u) \tag{1.2}$$

---

[1] In the absence of an unskilled wage category in the Japanese
statistics, we have followed the procedure applied by Anne Richards
Loup who used for this purpose data for workers with primary school or
not having attended school (a) aged 17 years or less and having had 1-
2 years of work experience and (b) aged 20-24 years and having had 2-3
years of work experience. Unskilled wages have been equated to the
simple average of wages in the two categories.

discount rate for physical capital and d is the rate of depreiciation.

In turn, the flow measure of capital intensity (k^f) can be expressed as in (1.3) where va refers to value added per man. Now, non-wage value added per man $(va_i - \bar{w}_i)$ is taken to represent physical capital-intensity and wage value added per man $(\bar{w}_i - w_i^u)$ human-capital intensity.

$$k_i^f = va_i - W_i^u = p_i^f + h_i^f = (va_i - \bar{w}_i) + (\bar{w}_i - w_i^u) \qquad (1.3)$$

As far as physical capital intensity is concerned, the two measures will give the same result in risk-free equilibrium, provided that product, capital, and labor markets are perfect and non-wage value added does not include any items other than capital remuneration. However, production is subject to risks that vary among industries, and, assuming risk aversion, profit rates will include a risk premium that will differ from industry to industry. Also, the situation in a particular year will not represent an equilibrium position and this fact, as well as imperfections in product, capital, and labor markets, will further contribute to interindustry variations in profits. Moreover, non-wage value added may include items other than capital's remuneration, such as advertising.

The existence of inter-industry differences in risk, market imperfections, and the inclusion of items other than capital's remuneration in non-wage value added, represent deficiencies of the flow measures of capital-intensity. In turn, the lack of consideration given to inter-industry differences in depreciation rates and in the extent of obsolesence of existing equipment, as well as the use of historical rather than replacement values for physical capital, represent disadvantages of the stock measure.

The implications of the described shortcomings of the two measures of capital-intensity for the results will depend on the particular circumstances of the situation. The usefulness of the stock measure would be greatly impaired in an inflationary situation where historical and replacement values differ and the magnitude of their differences varies with the age of equipment. This is not the case in the present study since the benchmark years chosen for estimating capital-intensity (1969

and 1970) in using U.S. and 1973 in using Japanese coefficients are part
of a long non-inflationary period. By contrast, the usefulness of the
flow measure is limited by reason of the fact that profit rates show
considerable variation over time and inter-industry differences in profit
rates cannot be fully explained by reference to risk factors.

1.4 Estimating Factor Endowments

Physical capital endowments have been estimated as the sum of gross fixed
investment over the preceding seventeen year period, expressed in constant
prices and converted into U.S. dollars at the 1963 exchange rate.
Investment values have been assumed to depreciate at an annual rate of 4
percent a year, so as to reflect the obsolescence of capital; such an
adjustment was not made in the earlier paper (Balassa, 1979b). Physical
capital endowments have been expressed in per capita terms.

A similar procedure was employed by Hufbauer, except that he used data for
the period 1953-64 and included manufacturing investment only (1970, p.
157). The choice of a longer period in the present study reflects the
fact that capital equipment is used beyond eleven years; also, we have
considered all capital, and not only that used in the manufacturing
sector. [1]

Hufbauer used the ratio of professional, technical, and related workers to
the labor force in manufacturing as a proxy for human capital endowment
(1970, p. 158). The use of this measure is objectionable, however,
because it includes various liberal occupations while excluding production
supervisors, foremen, and skilled workers who are of considerable
importance in the manufacturing sector.

A more appropriate procedure appears to be to make use of the Harbison-

---

[1] This choice can be rationalised on the grounds that, ex ante, capital
can be allocated to manufacturing as well as to other sectors. And
while adjustments would need to be made if there was complementarity
between capital and natural resources, as in mining, information on
the sectoral composition of investment was not available for a number
of the countries under study.

Myers index of human resource development. [1/] While this index is a flow
measure, [2/] the use of estimates with a six-year lag (Harbison, Maruhnic,
and Resnick, 1970, pp. 175-6) makes it possible to provide an indication
of a country's general educational level, and thus its human capital
base. We also experimented with the skill ratio employed by Hufbauer,
utilizing the data reported in the ILO <u>Yearbook of Labor Statistics</u>, but
the statistical results were much weaker and are not reported in this
study. [3/]

1.5 A Short Outline

Chapters 2 and 3 report on the results of the econometric analysis of
comparative advantage. Chapter 2 tests the Hechscher-Ohlin theory by the
simultaneous introduction of trade flows, factor intensities, and factor
endowments, taking the country as a unit of observation. In the same
chapter, the appropriateness of aggregating physical and human capital is
analyzed and an effort is made to explain the residuals of the estimating
equation through the introduction of additional variables. Furthermore,
estimates are made for a later year (1979) and the reliability of the
projections is investigated.

Chapter 3 uses trade flows between pairs of countries as the unit of
observation in testing the Hechscher-Ohlin theory. The multilateral model
is first applied to all the countries of the sample and, subsequently, to
trade among developed countries, among developing countries, between
developed and developing countries, and among European countries.

1/ This index was also used in a study of world trade flows by Gruber and
    Vernon (1970).

2/ It is derived as the secondary school enrolment rate plus five times
    the university enrolment rate in the respective age cohorts.

3/ For results obtained in an earlier investigation, see Balassa, 1979b.

Chapter 2

COMPARATIVE ADVANTAGE IN A MULTI-PRODUCT
AND MULTI-FACTOR MODEL
WITH COUNTRY OBSERVATIONS

2.1 A Two-Stage Model of Comparative Advantage

Balassa (1979b) introduced a two-stage procedure to analyze the pattern of
comparative advantage in manufactured products. In the first stage of
estimation, indices of comparative advantage for manufacturing product
categories were regressed on variables representing relative capital
intensity in the case of each country. In the second stage, the
regression coefficients obtained for the individual countries were
regressed on variables representing relative factor endowments in a cross-
section framework.

The method entails transposing results obtain in "commodity space" into
"country space," so as to indicate the effects of country characteristics
on international specialization in manufactured products. This contrasts
with the conventional procedure that involves using trade data for the
individual industries of a single country. Also, while the conventional
procedure infers the country's factor endowments from its trade pattern,
the two-stage procedure provides a test of the Heckscher-Ohlin theory of
comparative advantage by introducing factor endowments in the estimating
equation.

The first stage of estimation is respresented by equation (2.1), where
indices of comparative advantage (x_{ij}) are regressed on the capital-labor

Table 2.1

Number of Statistically Significant Regression Coefficients

in the First Stage Regression: U.S. Data, 1971

| | Export Equations | | Import Equations | | Net Export Equations | |
	Stock	Flow	Stock	Flow	Stock	Flow
1% level	14 14	12 11	16 16	19 19	25 22	26 25
5% level	20 19	20 19	20 20	20 20	29 23	29 26
10% level	24 22	22 20	22 20	23 23	30 24	29 26
Total No.	38 27[b]	38 22[b]	38 24[c]	38 26[c]	38 24[c]	38 26[c]

Note: (a) A two-tail test has been used in deriving levels of statistical significance.
       (b) Excluding coefficient values in the range (-.3, .3).
       (c) Excluding coefficient values in the range (-.15, .15).

ratio for product category i (k_i) , [1] defined as the sum of physical and human capital per worker, for each country j. A positive (negative) β coefficient indicates that a country has a comparative advantage in capital (labor) intensive products while the numerical magnitude of the β coefficient is interpreted to show the extent of the country's comparative advantage in capital (labor) intensive products.

$$\log x_{ij} = \alpha_j + \beta_j \log k_i \qquad\qquad\qquad (2.1)$$

In equation (2.2), the β coefficients thus obtained are regressed on measures of per capita physical capital (GDICAP) and human capital (HMIND) endowments, so as to test the hypothesis that intercountry differences in the β coefficients can be explained by differences in country characteristics. Other country characteristics, such as the level of development (defined by the use of a dummy variable) and per capita incomes have also been tried but did not give statistically significant results.

---

[1] On the disaggregation of the capital coefficient, see below.

$$\beta_j = a + b \text{ GDICAP}_j + c \text{ HMIND}_j . \qquad (2.2)$$

In subsequent work (Balassa, 1986, 1987), the two stages of calculation were combined through the application of a "one-pass" procedure. The relevant formulas are presented in Section 2.3.

Section 2.2 presents the results of the estimates utilizing the U.S. and Japanese coefficients described in Section 1.3. In Section 2.3, the implications of the disaggregation of the capital coefficients are indicated; Section 2.4 reports an attempt to explain the residuals of the estimates; and Section 2.5 examines the reliability of projections of comparative advantage. There is further a technical appendix.

2.2 The Estimation Results

Tables 2.1 and 2.2 show the number of statistically significant regression coefficients obtained in the first stage of estimation utilizing U.S. and Japanese data, respectively. The corresponding results for the second stage of estimation are presented in Tables 2.3 and 2.4.

In calculations made by the use of U.S. data, the regression coefficients obtained in the first stage of estimation are statistically significant at the 1 percent level in one-third of the export equations and in a large proportion of the import equations, utilizing a two-tail test. About six-tenths of the coefficients are significant at the 5 percent level in both the export and the import equations, with further items added at the 10 percent level of significance. Finally, about two-thirds of the coefficients are significant at the 1 percent level and about three-fourths at the 5 percent level in the net export equations. The results are somewhat stronger using Japanese data, especially at the 10 percent level of significance.

But coefficient values near to zero have an economic interpretation even if they are not significantly different from zero; they indicate that the country is at a dividing line as far as comparative advantage in capital- and in labor-intensive products is concerned. Correspondingly, Tables 2.1 and 2.2 also report significance levels excluding regression coefficients

Part I

Table 2.2

Number of Statistically Significant Regression Coefficients

in the First Stage Regressions: Japanese Data, 1977

	Export Equations				Import Equations				Net Export Equations			
	Stock		Flow		Stock		Flow		Stock		Flow	
1% level	14	13	12	10	21	21	21	21	29	25	21	21
5% level	23	20	20	27	25	23	22	22	32	26	27	25
10% level	29	23	21	18	27	24	24	24	32	26	31	26
Total No.	38	25^b	38	26^b	38	25^c	38	27^c	38	26^c	38	26^c

Note: (a) A two-tail test has been used in deriving levels of statistical significance.
       (b) Excluding coefficient values in the range (-. 3, .3)
       (c) Excluding coefficient values in the range (-. 15, .15)

that have values near to zero. The omission of these coefficients greatly
improves the statistical significance of the results. In the net export
equations, all the regression coefficients are now significant at the 1
percent level.

At the second stage of estimation, weighted least-squares have been used
in this study for purposes of eliminating heteroscedasticity in the place
of ordinary least-squares utilized in the earlier investigation.
Following Amemiya (1978), the reciprocals of the standard deviations of
the disturbances have been used as weights. 1/

The regression coefficients of the endowment variables have the expected
signs, positive for the export and the net export regressions and negative
for the, import regressions. If the endowment variables are introduced
separately in the regressions, they are statistically significant at the 1
percent level in all the regressions, with the t-values ranging between

---

1/ For greater detail on estimation procedures, see the Technical
    Appendix.

3.5 and 7.5. $\underline{1/}$

The level of statistical significance of the regression coefficients is reduced if the two endowment variables are introduced jointly in the same regression, reflecting intercorrelation between the two. Nevertheless, in the large majority of the cases, the regression coefficients of the endowment variables are highly significant statistically.

In the regressions utilizing U.S. data, the physical capital endowment variable is statistically significantly different from zero at the 1 percent level in all the equations, using a one-tail test. In the same regressions, the human capital variable is significant at the 1 percent level in the export equations, at the 5 percent level in the net export equations, but it is not significant in the import equations.

In the regressions using Japanese data, the regression coefficients of both endowment variables are statistically significant at least at the 5 percent level in the export equations, the exception being the human capital endowment variable that is significant at the 10 percent level, when the stock measure of capital intensity is used. In turn, the physical capital endowment variable is statistically significant at the 1 percent level in the import equations while the human capital endowment variable has the expected sign but it is not significant at even the 10 percent level. $\underline{2/}$ Finally, the regression coefficients of both endowment variables are significant at the 1 percent level in the net export equations, except that the human capital endowment variable is significant at only the 10 percent level in the equation utilizing the stock measure of capital intensity.

On the whole, the best statistical results have been obtained in the net export equations, possibly indicating the existence of compensating errors in the export and import data. In turn, by far the poorest results have

---

$\underline{1/}$ To economize with space, these results are not reported.

$\underline{2/}$ The lower statistical significance of the coefficients of the human capital endowment variable may be attributed to errors in measurement.

Part I

Table 2.3

Explanation of Intercountry Differences in the
Pattern of Specialization in Manufactured Goods
U.S. Data, 1971

	Constant	Physical Capital Endowment	Human Capital Endowment	$\bar{R}^2$
Two-Stage Estimation				
Export Equations				
stock variables	-1.16 (8.48)	1.07 (2.76)	0.45 (2.96)	0.6813
flow variables	-1.07 (7.87)	0.93 (2.43)	0.46 (3.10)	0.6380
Import Equations				
stock variables	1.03 (5.90)	-1.78 (3.51)	-0.07 (0.34)	0.5995
flow variables	1.01 (6.31)	-1.62 (3.51)	-0.09 (0.47)	0.6284
Net Export Equations				
stock variables	-0.45 (10.11)	0.66 (4.99)	0.10 (1.91)	0.7899
flow variables	-0.44 (10.26)	0.57 (4.52)	0.12 (2.38)	0.7862
"One-Pass" Estimation				$\hat{\sigma}$
Export Equations				
stock variables	-0.99 (7.48)	0.47 (5.31)	0.28 (3.83)	0.48
flow variables	-0.90 (6.57)	0.90 (4.81)	0.28 (3.79)	0.48
Import Equations				
stock variables	0.78 (9.05)	-0.79 (6.66)	-0.06 (1.35)	0.56
flow variables	0.77 (8.61)	-0.67 (5.53)	-0.07 (1.52)	0.57
Net Export Equations				
stock variables	-0.40 (13.84)	0.50 (10.10)	0.08 (4.92)	0.47
flow variables	-0.39 (12.80)	0.43 (8.50)	0.10 (4.80)	0.47

Note: For explanation see text; t-values shown in parenthesis.
σ = residual variance.

been obtained in the import equations, where the idiosyncrasies of national protection enter.

These results are reflected in the adjusted coefficients of determination. In calculations made with U.S. data, nearly four-fifths of the variance in the β -coefficients estimated in the first stage is explained by intercountry differences in physical and human capital endowments in the net export equations; the corresponding proportions are two-thirds and three-fifths in the export and import equations, respectively.

The coefficient of determination is also the highest in the net export equations estimated by the use of Japanese data. Approximately three-fourths of the variance of the β coefficients is explained by intercountry differences in capital endowments. However, the explanatory power of the import equation is greater than that of the export equation. In the first case, over three-fifths of the variance of the β -coefficients is explained by intercountry differences in capital endowments, irrespective of the choice of the measure of capital intensity; in the second case, the coefficients of determination are 0.59 and 0.45 in the equations incorporating the stock and the flow measures of capital intensity, respectively.

Apart from the import equations, the statistical results obtained by the use of U.S. data tend to be stronger than those obtained by the use of Japanese data. Possible explanations are the superior quality of U.S. data and the larger industry sample available in the United States (167 commodity categories) than in Japan (97 categories).

Calculations have further been made by combining the estimation of the two stages through the application of a "one-pass" procedure. This has been done by utilizing the error component model (ECM) which involves introducing an industry-specific error term in addition to a country

Table 2.4

Explanation of Intercountry Differences
in the Pattern of Specialization in Manufactured Goods: Japanese Data, 1973

	Constant		Physical Capital Endowment		Human Capital Endowment		$\bar{R}^2$
Two-Stage Estimation							
Export Equations							
stock variables	−1.35	(6.51)	1.70	(2.83)	0.33	(1.40)	0.5947
flow variables	−1.09	(5.28)	1.10	(1.88)	0.43	(1.84)	0.4467
Import Equations							
stock variables	0.92	(6.21)	−1.58	(3.66)	−0.04	(0.24)	0.6261
flow variables	0.99	(6.30)	−1.42	(3.08)	−0.14	(0.77)	0.6075
Net Export Equations							
stock variables	−0.50	(8.99)	0.79	(4.88)	0.08	(1.27)	0.7597
flow variables	−0.49	(9.24)	0.62	(3.98)	0.15	(2.35)	0.7425
"One-Pass" Estimation							$\hat{\sigma}$
Export Equations							
stock variables	−1.30	(10.00)	1.61	(7.41)	0.27	(3.17)	4.03
flow variables	−1.14	(6.82)	1.25	(4.46)	0.42	(3.74)	4.18
Import Equations							
stock variables	0.86	(9.87)	−1.29	(9.38)	−0.03	(0.53)	1.63
flow variables	1.00	(9.32)	−1.35	(7.85)	−0.12	(1.81)	1.66
Net Export Equations							
stock variables	−0.49	(16.00)	0.73	(12.00)	0.08	(3.39)	0.31
Flow variables	−0.50	(12.60)	0.62	(8.24)	0.15	(4.85)	0.32

Note: For explanation see text; t-values are shown in parenthesis.
      σ = residual variance

specific error term. [1]

The use of the error component method gives similar coefficient values as the two-stage estimation, but it generally raises the statistical significance of the coefficients to a considerable extent. The levels of significance exceed 1 percent, except for the human capital endowment

1/ For a detailed discussion, see the Technical Appendix to this chapter.

variable in the import equation, where this variable is not statistically significant in the U.S. regressions; it is significant at the 10 percent level utilizing the flow measure and it does not reach acceptable levels of significance utilizing the stock measure of capital in the regressions using Japanese data.

The higher levels of significance under "one-pass" estimation are explained by the fact that combining the two stages increases the number of observations in the estimating equation. And while this method does not permit deriving the coefficient of determination, in terms of the goodness of fit the net export equations place first, followed by the export and by the import equations.

2.3 Alternative Specifications of the Capital Coefficient

The results reported so far have been derived by aggregating physical and human capital intensity into a single measure of capital. In the following, the appropriateness of this procedure will be tested by the use of the one-pass procedure.

Equations (2.3) to (2.5) provide the derivation of the one-pass equation for the case when physical (p) and human capital (h) are separately introduced. The estimation has been done by OLS, corrected for heteroscedascity, which represents an alternative to the error component model utilized in Tables 2.3 and 2.4. The estimates have been obtained by the use of U.S. data and pertain to net exports (NNX_{ij}).

$$NNX_{ij} = \alpha_j + \beta_{pj}\ln p_i + \beta_{hj} \ln h_i + u_{ij} \tag{2.3}$$

$$\beta_{pj} = a_p + b_p G_j + v_{pj} \tag{2.4a}$$

$$\beta_{hj} = a_h + b_h H_j + v_{hj} \tag{2.4b}$$

$$NNX_{ij} = \alpha_j + a_p \ln p_i + a_h \ln h_i \tag{2.5}$$

$$+ b_p G_j \ln p_i + b_h H_j \ln h_i + \varepsilon_{ij}, \text{ where}$$

$$\varepsilon_{ij} = v_{pj} \ln p_i + v_{hi} \ln h_i + u_{ij}.$$

A comparison of (2.4) and (2.5) shows that one can interpret the coefficients of $\ln p_i$ and $\ln h_i$ in one-pass estimation as the constants of the second-stage equation and the coefficients of $G_j \ln p_i$ and $H_j \ln h_i$ as the coefficients of G_j and H_j in the second-stage equation. Under certain assumptions the two sets of estimated coefficients will have equal values (Amemiya, 1978), although their levels of statistical significance will differ owing to differences in the number of observations.

In the equations, u_{ij} is the error terms in (2.3), v_{pj} and v_{hj} are the error terms in (2.4), and ε_{ij} the error term in (2.5). The latter term will be heteroscedastic even if u_{ij}, v_{pj}, and v_{hj} are assumed to be homoscedastic. We have estimated (2.5) by ordinary least squares (OLS), assuming ε_{ij} to be heteroscedastic, with a variance of an unknown form. However, adjustment of the t-statistics has been made for the unknown form of heteroscedasticity by the use of a procedure proposed by White (1980).

The results are reported in Table 2.5. The regression coefficients of the capital endowment variables have the expected sign and all the coefficients, as well as the constants of the regression equations, are statistically significant at the 1 percent level.

The aggregation of capital does not affect the statistical significance of the estimated coefficients; nor does aggregation affect the explanatory power of the regression equations, with the coefficients of determination being in the 0.46-0.47 range in both cases. This result contrasts with that obtained by several authors (Branson, 1973; Stern, 1976; Branson and Monoyios, 1977; and Stern and Maskus, 1981). However, in the latter studies differences in the signs of physical and human capital were shown for two industrial countries at the upper end of the distribution, the United States and Germany. Also, as noted in Chapter 1, the interpretation of the estimates of these authors is open to question because capital endowments were inferred from estimates pertaining to capital intensities.

Table 2.5

Explanation of Intercountry Differences in the Pattern of Specialization

in Manufactured Goods

(OLS estimates, with t-values adjusted for heteroscedasticity in parentheses)

Equations	$\ln k_i$	$\ln p_i$	$\ln h_i$	$G_j \ln k_i$	$H_j \ln k_i$	$G_j \ln p_i$	$H_j \ln h_i$	$\bar{R}^2$
Stock	−0.47			0.68	0.10			.4704
	(18.74)			(9.89)	(3.72)			.4626
Flow	−0.46			0.60	0.12			.4626
	(16.32)			(8.05)	(4.11)			
Stock		−0.21	−0.26			0.45	0.17	.4675
		(12.64)	(11.74)			(10.28)	(10.21)	
Flow		−0.21	−0.29			0.43	0.18	.4618
		(9.16)	(12.56)			(7.80)	(11.01)	

Note: For explanation of symbols, see text.

2.4 Explaining the Residuals

A further question concerns the explanation of the residuals of the equations reported in Tables 2.3 and 2.4. In two stage estimation, for example, there are differences between the values of the β coefficients estimated in the first stage and the fitted values of the coefficients derived in the second stage of estimation. [1] More specifically, we wish to explain why some countries export (import) more -- and others less -- capital intensive products than would be expected on the basis of their physical and human capital endowments.

A possible explanatory factor is the trade policies applied by the individual countries. Notwithstanding the research efforts undertaken over the past fifteen years, however, we do not have comparable import protection figures for developing countries. This is largely because of

---

[1] This distinction between estimated and fitted values of the coefficients will be used throughout in the following.

the use of quantitative import restrictions by these countries, the tariff equivalent of which is difficult to measure. Also, protection levels change over time and the estimates soon become outdated.

We have, therefore, measured trade orientation in an indirect way, defining it in terms of deviations of observed from hypothetical values of per capita exports. Hypothetical values have been derived as the fitted values of a regression equation that, in addition to the per capita income and population variables utilized in early work by Chenery (1960), includes variables representing the availability of mineral resources and propinquity to foreign markets. The latter two variables have been included in the expectation that, ceteris paribus, the availability of mineral resources and propinquity will raise per capita exports. [1]

Mineral resource availability has been represented by the ratio of mineral exports to the gross domestic product while propinquity has been defined as the weighted average of the inverse of the distance between the country concerned and the other 37 countries included in the investigation, the weights being the gross national products of the partner countries. The results are reported in equation (2.6), where X is the value of total exports,

$$\log (X_j/P_j) = 0.1864 + 0.9212 \log (Y_j/P_j) - 0.3541 \log P_j \qquad (2.6)$$
$$ (0.38) \quad (15.02) (6.38)$$

$$+ 0.0251 \ X_j^m/Y_j + 0.0598 \sum_k \frac{Y_{jk}/D_{jk}}{\Sigma Y_k} \ ; \ R^2 = 0.9404$$
$$ (2.91) (2.06)$$

Y the gross national product, P population, X^m mineral exports, D_{jk} average distance from the market of country k and j refers to the country. The equation has been estimated for the year 1971. The equation

---

[1] The described procedure has first been utilized in Balassa, 1985; a distance variable has been added in the present paper. While population appears in the terms shown on the two sides of the equation, as in Chenery's original formulation, and mineral exports are included in total exports, this should not affect the appropriateness of using deviations from hypothetical values as an indication of trade orientation.

has a high explanatory power and all the regression coefficients are statistically significant at the 1 percent level.

In utilizing the results for the purpose at hand, it has been hypothesized that upward (downward) deviations of actual from predicted values of per capita exports would be associated with downward (upward) deviations in regard to the fitted β coefficients in the export and net export equations and upward (downward) deviations in the import equations. This is because the results are dominated by the developing countries, where the deviations from the regression line in the second-stage equations and the deviations from the regression line in the trade-orientation equation are several times greater than that for the developed countries. [1] At the same time, in the developing countries, a low degree of openness can be expected to be associated with the capital-intensity of exports (imports) being above (below) its predicted value. In fact, the largest upward (downward) deviations in the export and net export (import) equations are shown in developing countries with relatively high protection, such as Argentina, Brazil, and Mexico and downward deviations in developing countries with relatively low protection, such as Hong Kong and Korea.

Deviations between estimated and fitted values of the β coefficients may also depend on the commodity concentration of exports. It has been hypothesized that export concentration (diversification) will favor (retard) the exploitation of the country's comparative advantage. With protection in developing countries hindering specialization in products in which a country has a comparative advantage, it may be expected that export concentration would give rise to negative (positive) deviations in

---

[1] In the export equation utilizing the flow measure of capital intensity, the standard deviation of the unweighted residuals is two-and-a-half times, in the trade orientation equations three times, higher for developing countries than for developed countries.

the export and net export (import) equations. [1]

Another variable used to explain differences between estimated and fitted values is foreign direct investment.   It has been suggested that foreign direct investment in developing countries is biased towards capital intensive activities.   Correspondingly, it may be hypothesized that foreign direct investment would give rise to positive (negative) deviations in the export and net export (import) equations. [2]   The foreign direct investment variable has been measured by cumulating balance-of-payments data deflated by the price index of world export unit values for a ten year period preceding the year of estimation.

While in the above discussion reference was made to differences between the values of the β coefficients estimated in the first stage and the fitted values derived from the second stage, the results can be reinterpreted in terms of "one-pass" estimation.   The general statement will apply in this case: we try to explain why some countries export (import) more -- and others less -- capital intensive products that can be expected on the basis of their physical and human capital endowment.

Tables 2.6 and 2.7 report the best statistical estimates that include the trade orientation variable in the export equation and the export concentration and foreign direct investment variables in the import and the net export equations.   The regression coefficients have the expected sign and are statistically significant at the 1 percent level in all the equations obtained by the use of Japanese data and in most of the equations obtained by the use of U.S. data.

The correct sign and the high statistical significance of the variables in the regression equations explaining the residuals of the second-stage

---

1/ Export concentration has been measured by utilizing the Herfindahl index.

2/ While direct foreign investment is used here as an explanatory variable, Baldwin has tried to explain the pattern of U.S. direct foreign investment using the same explanatory variables as those employed in explaining the U.S. pattern of trade (1977).

Table 2.6

Explanation of Residuals in Equation Explaining Inter-Country Differences in the Pattern of Specialization in Manufactured Goods, U.S. Data (1971)

	Foreign Direct Trade Orientation	Export Concentration	Investment	$\bar{R}^2$
Two-Stage Estimation				
Export Equation				
stock variables	−0.33 (2.40)	−	−	0.1342
flow variables	−0.26 (1.83)	−	−	0.0833
Import Equation				
stock variables	−	4.03 (3.03)	−0.03 (2.00)	0.1901
flow variables	−	3.98 (3.36)	−0.04 (2.18)	0.2254
Net Export Equations				
stock variables	−	−0.60 (1.57)	0.01 (1.33)	0.0422
flow variables	−	−0.67 (1.85)	0.01 (1.43)	0.0651
"One-Pass" Estimation				
Export Equations				
stock variables	−0.33 (2.32)	−	−	0.1265
flow variables	−0.26 (1.77)	−	−	0.0778
Import Equations				
stock variables	−	5.02 (3.43)	−0.05 (2.82)	0.2404
flow variables	−	4.94 (3.70)	−0.05 (3.05)	0.2714
Net Export Equations				
stock variables	−	−0.79 (2.01)	−0.01 (2.06)	0.1244
flow variables	−	−0.85 (2.29)	−0.01 (2.19)	0.1474

Note: For explanation see text; t-values are shown in parenthesis.

Table 2.7

Explanation of Residuals in Equation Explaining
Inter-Country Differences in the Pattern of Specialization
Japanese Data (1973)

	Trade Orientation	Export Concentration	Foreign Direct Investment	$\bar{R}^2$
Two-Stage Estimation				
Export Equation				
stock variables	-0.51 (2.56)	- -	- -	0.1502
flow variables	-0.65 (3.45)	- -	- -	0.2429
Import Equation				
stock variables	- -	3.93 (3.58)	-0.04 (2.50)	0.2522
flow variables	- -	4.59 (3.88)	-0.04 (2.74)	0.2863
Net Export Equations				
stock variables	- -·	-1.10 (2.52)	0.01 (2.51)	0.1543
flow variables	- -	-1.00 (2.37)	0.01 (2.56)	0.1311
"One-Pass" Estimation				
Export Equations				
stock variables	-0.51 (2.53)	- -	- -	0.1474
flow variables	-0.63 (3.35)	- -	- -	0.2323
Import Equations				
stock variables	- -	4.15 (3.74)	-0.04 (3.06)	0.2753
flow variables	- -	4.94 (3.85)	-0.05 (3.11)	0.2870
Net Export Equations				
stock variables	- -	-0.79 (2.65)	-0.02 (2.81)	0.1815
flow variables	- -	-0.85 (2.27)	-0.01 (2.45)	0.1373

Note: For explanation see text; t-values are shown in parenthesis.

equations confirm the suggested hypotheses, when the trade orientation and
the export concentration variables may be regarded as alternative
indicators of the trade policies applied.   At the same time, the low

coefficients of determination indicate the existence of random elements in the results. This is hardly surprising, given that the dependent variable is a residual from the previous regression.

Estimates have further been made by combining the factor endowment variables and the variables used to explain the residuals of the second-stage equations in a single set of equations. Most of the combined equations have considerably higher coefficients of determination, reflecting the advantages of combining the two sets of variables. At the same time, while the t-values for the coefficients of the endowment variables tend to be lower, their level of statistical significance is hardly affected. This conclusion also applies to the variables used to explain the residuals of the second-stage equations, except that the foreign direct investment variable in the import equation and the export concentration variable in the net export equation lose their statistical significance (Tables 2.8 and 2.9).

The t-values for the coefficients of the endowment variables also decrease in the case when these variables are combined with the variables explaining the residuals in the form of "one-pass" estimation but, apart from the human capital endowment variable in the import equation using the flow measure of capital, all the regression coefficients retain their statistical significance. In turn, the t-values for the variables explaining the residuals rise in several cases and the trade orientation variable now enters into the net export equation. These results are of particular interest since combining the two stages of estimation and the variables used in explaining the residuals may be considered superior to their separate estimation.

2.5 Projecting into the Future

In an earlier paper, it was suggested that "the results can further be utilized to gauge the direction in which a country's comparative advantage is moving ... by substituting projected future values of a country's physical and human capital endowments in the intercountry regressions, so as to estimate prospective values of the β coefficients (Balassa, 1979a,

Table 2.8

Combined Explanation of Intercountry Differences in
the Pattern of Specialization in Manufactured Goods, U.S. Data (1971)

	Constant	Physical Capital Endowment	Human Capital Endowment	Trade Orientation	Export Concentration	Foreign Direct Investment	$\bar{R}^2$
Two-Stage Estimation							
Export Equations							
stock variables	-1.13 (8.55)	1.02 (2.72)	0.45 (3.12)	-0.31 (2.06)	—	—	0.7082
flow variables	-1.05 (7.77)	0.89 (2.36)	0.47 (3.17)	-0.23 (1.51)	—	—	0.6509
Import Equations							
stock variables	0.73 (2.34)	-1.94 (3.59)	-0.02 (0.10)	—	5.02 (2.77)	-0.00 (0.05)	0.7132
flow variables	0.72 (2.61)	-1.81 (3.77)	-0.04 (0.22)	—	4.89 (3.05)	-0.00 (0.03)	0.7505
Net Export Equations							
stock variables	-0.49 (5.16)	0.56 (3.40)	0.01 (1.77)	—	-0.38 (0.70)	0.02 (1.22)	0.7854
flow variables	-0.49 (5.16)	0.44 (2.85)	0.13 (2.39)	—	-0.42 (0.82)	0.02 (1.46)	0.7919
"One-Pass" Estimation							$\hat{\sigma}$
Export Equations							
stock variables	-0.97 (7.36)	0.92 (4.98)	0.29 (3.96)	-0.19 (2.83)	—	—	0.28
flow variables	-0.89 (6.49)	0.86 (4.56)	0.29 (3.89)	-0.14 (2.10)	—	—	0.28
Import Equations							
stock variables	0.69 (5.91)	-0.84 (5.74)	-0.04 (0.91)	—	2.11 (4.34)	-0.00 (0.29)	0.38
flow variables	0.69 (5.76)	-0.71 (4.75)	-0.06 (1.12)	—	1.87 (3.80)	-0.00 (0.28)	0.39
Net Export Equations							
stock variables	-0.42 (10.10)	0.43 (7.55)	0.08 (4.13)	-0.02 (1.34)	-0.45 (2.23)	0.01 (2.68)	0.23
flow variables	-0.42 (9.51)	0.37 (6.29)	0.09 (4.56)	-0.01 (2.71)	-0.48 (2.33)	0.01 (2.86)	0.23

Note: For explanation see text; t-values shown in parenthesis.

Table 2.9

Combined Estimation of Explanation of Intercountry Differences
in the Pattern of Specialization in Manufactured Goods, Japanese Data (1973)

	Constant	Physical Capital Endowment	Human Capital Endowment	Trade Orientation	Export Concentration	Foreign Direct Investment	$\bar{R}^2$
Two-Stage Estimation							
Export Equations							
stock variables	-1.30 (6.59)	1.58 (2.80)	0.35 (1.55)	-0.51 (2.39)	– –	– –	0.6426
flow variables	-1.02 (5.48)	0.97 (1.83)	0.44 (2.11)	-0.64 (3.08)	– –	– –	0.5545
Import Equations							
stock variables	0.87 (3.40)	-1.52 (3.41)	-0.01 (0.06)	– –	3.79 (2.53)	-0.04 (1.08)	0.7490
flow variables	0.93 (3.43)	-1.36 (2.89)	-0.10 (0.61)	– –	4.31 (2.72)	-0.04 (1.13)	0.7399
Net Export Equations							
stock variables	-0.59 (5.58)	0.64 (3.52)	0.07 (1.08)	– –	-0.68 (1.12)	0.03 (2.37)	0.8006
flow variables	-0.55 (5.38)	0.54 (3.09)	0.12 (1.99)	– –	-0.69 (1.17)	0.03 (1.92)	0.7791
							$\hat{\sigma}$
"One-Pass" Estimation							
Export Equations							
stock variables	-1.27 (9.73)	1.52 (6.91)	0.29 (3.38)	-0.39 (4.87)	– –	– –	4.05
flow variables	-1.09 (6.48)	1.09 (3.87)	0.44 (3.98)	-0.58 (5.66)	– –	– –	4.19
Import Equations							
stock variables	0.83 (6.64)	-1.24 (7.28)	-0.01 (0.15)	– –	2.99 (5.31)	-0.03 (2.37)	1.66
flow variables	0.92 (5.95)	-1.26 (5.96)	-0.09 (1.28)	– –	4.07 (5.82)	-0.04 (2.42)	1.73
Net Export Equations							
stock variables	-0.56 (1.15)	0.59 (7.88)	0.07 (2.72)	– –	-0.70 (2.86)	0.03 (5.37)	0.31
flow variables	-0.55 (8.80)	0.54 (5.86)	0.12 (3.90)	– –	-0.74 (2.41)	0.03 (3.55)	0.32

Note: For explanation see text; t-values are shown in parenthesis.

p. 265). In turn, Bowen recommended caution "in using cross-section coefficients as a basis for inferring likely time-series behavior" (1983, p. 407), with particular reference to the above suggestion.

In this study, projections have been made by utilizing estimates for 1971 [1]/ and 1979; the latter estimates have been derived by applying the coefficients used earlier to 1979 trade flows. The projections have involved the use of two alternative procedures. Under the first method, we have projected the β coefficients by substituting the values taken by each country's endowment variables in 1979, adjusted for changes in average endowments for the entire group of countries, [2]/ into the second-stage equation for 1971, and we have compared the resulting projected β coefficients with the fitted β coefficients derived from the 1979 second-stage equations. Under the second method, we have added the residuals of the second stage equation to the projected β coefficients derived by the first method, and compared the resulting coefficients with the β coefficients estimated in the first-stage equation for 1979. [3]/ A detailed example is provided in the Technical Appendix to this chapter.

The results obtained with the first method show that the projected and estimated values are very close, with the coefficients of determination equal to 0.99 in all cases. The statistical results are slightly weaker under the second method, with the coefficients of determination being between 0.83 and 0.90. This is hardly surprising, given the variability of the difference between the values of the β coefficients estimated in the first-stage and the second-stage equations.

The results indicate the high predictive power of the estimates derived by

---

1/ 1973 for Japan.

2/ See equation (III) in the Technical Appendix to this chapter.

3/ The adjustment means that in the second case we effectively compare estimates from first-stage equations. This conforms to the statement made in the earlier paper, according to which "these projections further need to be adjusted in cases when observed values of the β coefficients differ from values estimated from the intercountry regression" (1979a, p. 265).

the methods utilized in the study. The slope coefficients are generally close to one, with a range from 0.81 to 1.01, and the constants very near to zero, ranging from -0.04 to 0.08. The first method gives a particularly good fit; while this could not have been expected from the second method, the results are quite close.

This is apparent in Figures 2.1 to 2.4 which show results pertaining to the export equations estimated by using the flow measure of capital intensity. Figures 2.1 and 2.2 have been derived using U.S., Figures 2.3 and 2.4 using Japanese, data. For definitions, see the Technical Appendix to this chapter.

It appears, then, that the estimates obtained in the cross-country framework can be utilized to project the trade structure of the individual countries as their factor endowments change.

Use has further been made of the method proposed by Bowen (1983), which entails relating changes in the factor content of trade to changes in factor endowments. This has involved regressing the differences between the β coefficients estimated for 1979 and for 1971 on differences in the endowment variables. The regression coefficients of changes in the endowment variables are statistically significant at the 1 percent level under both alternatives, and the coefficient of determination is in the 0.42 - 0.47 range.

2.6 Summary

This chapter has examined the pattern of comparative advantage in trade in manufactured goods in an intercountry framework. This has been done, to begin with, by utilizing a two-stage procedure. In the first stage, trade performance indicators have been related to the capital intensity of the individual product categories for each country; in the second stage, the regression coefficients thus obtained have been correlated with country endowment variables.

The empirical estimates show that intercountry differences in the structure of trade in manufactured goods are largely explained by

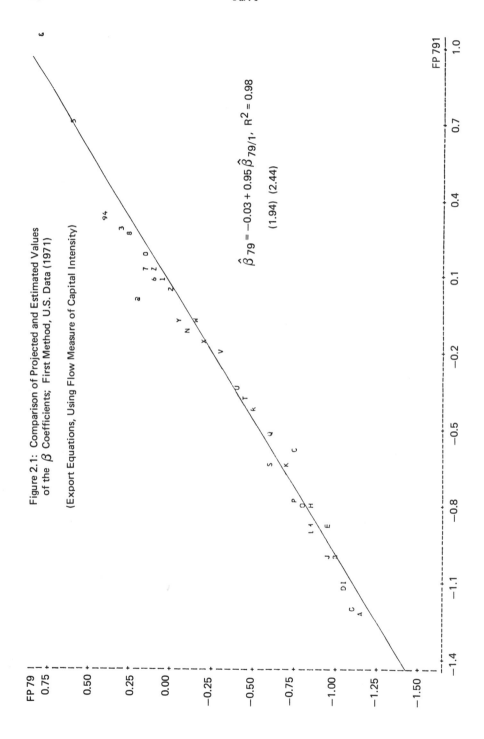

Figure 2.1: Comparison of Projected and Estimated Values
of the β Coefficients; First Method, U.S. Data (1971)

(Export Equations, Using Flow Measure of Capital Intensity)

$$\hat{\beta}_{79} = -0.03 + 0.95\,\hat{\beta}_{79/1}, \quad R^2 = 0.98$$
$$(1.94)\ (2.44)$$

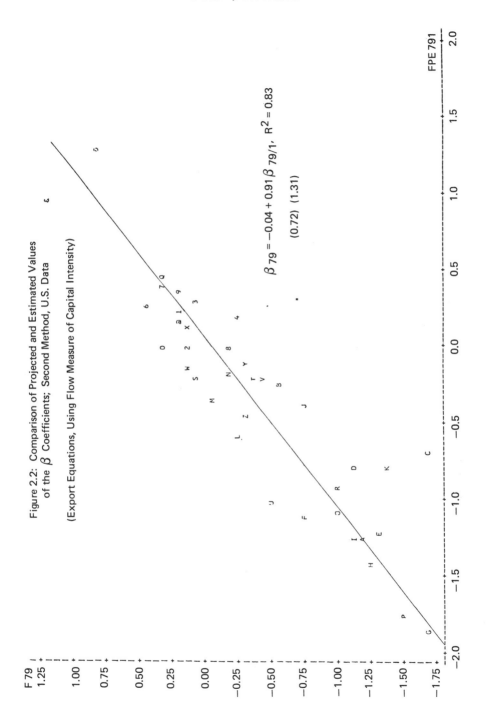

Figure 2.2: Comparison of Projected and Estimated Values
of the β Coefficients; Second Method, U.S. Data

(Export Equations, Using Flow Measure of Capital Intensity)

$$\beta_{79} = -0.04 + 0.91\,\beta_{79/1}, \quad R^2 = 0.83$$
$$(0.72)\ (1.31)$$

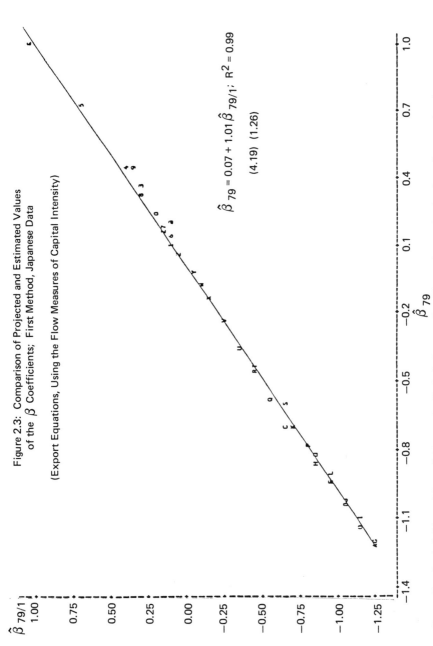

Figure 2.3: Comparison of Projected and Estimated Values of the β Coefficients; First Method, Japanese Data

(Export Equations, Using the Flow Measures of Capital Intensity)

$$\hat{\beta}_{79} = 0.07 + 1.01\,\hat{\beta}_{79/1}; \quad R^2 = 0.99$$
$$(4.19) \quad (1.26)$$

Note: For the definition of the variable, see the Technical Appendix. The t-values under the slope (intercept) estimates test whether the slope (intercept) is equal to 1 (0). The solid line traced is the diagonal.

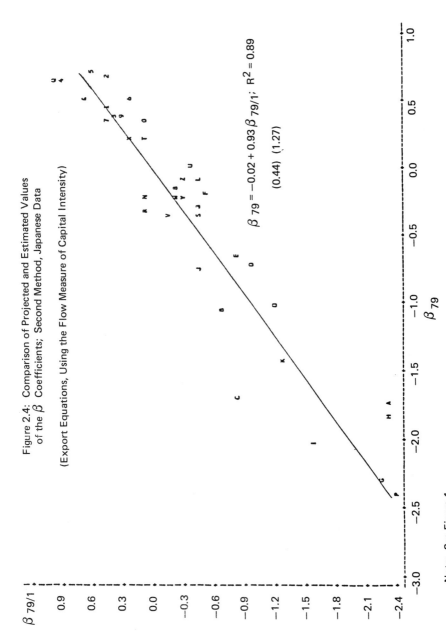

Figure 2.4: Comparison of Projected and Estimated Values of the β Coefficients; Second Method, Japanese Data

(Export Equations, Using the Flow Measure of Capital Intensity)

$$\beta_{79} = -0.02 + 0.93 \, \beta_{79/1}; \quad R^2 = 0.89$$
$$(0.44) \quad (1.27)$$

Note: See Figure 1.

differences in physical and human capital endowments. Each of the two endowment variables, taken alone, is statistically significant at the 1 percent level in all the regressions. The extent of statistical significance is reduced when they are introduced jointly in the regression equations, reflecting intercorrelation between the two in particular as far as the human capital endowment variable is concerned.

The best statistical results have been obtained in the net export equations, which provide in theory the most appropriate measure of comparative advantage. At the same time, taking the difference between exports and imports reduces the measurement errors associated with each. With one exception, all coefficients of the endowment variables are statistically significant at the 1 percent level and three-fourths of the variance of the β coefficients, derived at the first stage, is explained by intercountry differences in the endowment variables.

The statistical results improve further if a one-pass procedure is employed that combines the two stages of estimation. And while this method does not permit deriving the coefficient of determination, the residual variance is again the smallest in the net export equations.

It has further been attempted to explain the residuals in the second stage of estimation, pointing to the existence of differences between the country's actual and predicted trade patterns. This has been done by reference to variables such as the extent of trade orientation, the concentration of the export structure, and foreign direct investment, when the first two variables provide alternative indicators of trade policy. The regression coefficients of the trade policy orientation variable in the export equation and those of the export concentration and foreign direct investment variables in the import and net export equations have been found to be statistically significant at the 1 percent level, although the explanatory power of the equations is relatively low, probably reflecting measurement errors in the capital intensity and capital endowment variables used in the estimation. Similar results have been obtained by the use of one-pass estimates.

The level of statistical significance of the regression coefficients is somewhat lower if the endowment variables and the variables used in explaining the residuals are combined in a single second-stage equation, but the explanatory power of this regression is substantially higher than that of the original second-stage equation.   Finally, combining the two sets of explanatory variables generally improve the statistical results obtained under the one-pass procedure.

The chapter has also made comparisons between values of the β coefficients projected from the 1971 equations and estimated values from the 1979 equations.   The error of projection is small, irrespective of the choice of the projection method utilized.   It would appear, then, that the results obtained in cross-section estimation may be used to make projections for individual countries.

More generally, the cross-section results can be interpreted in a time-series framework.   They indicate that the accumulation of physical and human capital leads to shifts in export composition in the manufacturing sector from labor-intensive to physical and human capital-intensive products.   The application of this "stages approach" to international specialization (Balassa, 1979b), then, permits one to gauge changes in export composition in the process of economic development.

Technical Appendix

Several alternative estimation methods have been employed to analyse the
pattern of comparative advantage in manufactured goods in the present
study.   This appendix briefly describes the methods used in deriving the
estimates reported in the tables: a two-stage procedure using weighted
least-squares in the second stage of estimation and a one-pass procedure
using the error component model.   It will further describe the methods
used in projecting the β coefficients.

Estimation Methods

In two-stage estimation, weighted least-squares (WLS) have been used in
the second stage in order to adjust for heteroscedasticity by utilizing
the methodology proposed by Amemiya (1978).   The following assumptions
have been made in applying this methodology in the present investigation.

(a) the disturbances of the first-stage regressions are uncorrelated
     across countries; and

(b) the disturbances of the theoretical second-stage regression (i.e.
     the regression of the true. unknown, β coefficients, rather than
     the estimated $\hat{\beta}_j$'s of the first stage) are homoscedastic, are
     uncorrelated across countries, and are also uncorrelated with the
     disturbances of the first-stage regressions;

Under these assumptions, it can be shown that the disturbances of the
estimated second-stage regression (i.e. of the $\hat{\beta}_j$'s)   are still
uncorrelated, but are heteroscedastic, with a variance equal to the sum of
the variance of the $\hat{\beta}_j$ coefficients of the first-stage regressions and
the variance of the disturbances of the theoretical second-stage
regression.   The first variance (σ^2) is proportional to the variance of
the disturbances of the corresponding first-stage regression $\underline{1/}$ and
reflects the variability of the dependent variable of the first-stage

---

$\underline{1/}$ The proportionality factor is the inverse of the variance of the
     explanatory variable (the log of the sectoral technical coefficients)
     used in the first stage.

regression across countries. The second variance (W^2) reflects the fact that even if they were observable, the true β_j coefficients would not be perfectly determined by the explanatory variables used in the second stage. [1]

In practice, these two variances are not known, but are replaced by their OLS estimates, as suggested by Amemiya. Hence, to apply the described method, we use OLS and then run an additional regression in the second stage by WLS, with weights equal to $1/\sqrt{\hat{\sigma}^2 + \hat{W}^2}$ [2], the inverse of the estimated standard deviation of the disturbances of the estimated second-stage regression.

It is also shown by Amemiya that a one-pass procedure gives the same results as the two-stage procedure, based on the same hypotheses, when using a generalized least-squares estimator, which would reduce to a WLS estimator in our case, because of assumption a). In the underlying calculations made in the present study, one-pass estimation has been done by an error component model (ECM).

In an ECM, the disturbance is decomposed into three parts:

1) a country specific random effect α_j ; the α_j's are assumed to have a common constant variance σ_α^2 and be uncorrelated with one another, and with the w_i's and the ε_{ij}'s ;

2) an industry specific random effect w_i ; the w_i's are assumed to have a common constant variance σ_w^2 and be uncorrelated with one another and the ε_{ij}'s , and

3) a general effect ε_{ij}, with variance σ^2 .

---

[1] In an earlier paper (Balassa, 1979b), a correction for heteroscedasticity was made which takes account of the first variance but not of the second.

[2] If the second variance dominates the first variance, WLS will provide second-stage results very similar to OLS second-stage results. In the present study, this turned out to be the case, especially in the export and net export equations.

The explanatory variables consist of the ratrix premultiplying the vector (d a b c)' in (I). They include a sector specific effect (the log k column) and two cross effects (log k . $GDICAP_i$ and log k . $HMIND_i$), but no country specific effects. [1]/

$$
\begin{bmatrix} y_1 \\ y_2 \\ \cdot \\ \cdot \\ \cdot \\ y_N \end{bmatrix} = \begin{bmatrix} \iota & \log k & \log k \cdot GDICAP_1 & \log k \cdot HMIND_1 \\ \iota & \log k & \log k \cdot GDICAP_2 & \log k \cdot HMIND_2 \\ \cdot & & \cdot & \cdot \\ \cdot & & \cdot & \cdot \\ \cdot & & \cdot & \cdot \\ \iota & \log k & \log k \cdot GDICAP_N & \log k \cdot HMIND_N \end{bmatrix} \begin{bmatrix} d \\ a \\ b \\ c \end{bmatrix} + \begin{bmatrix} \iota\alpha_1 + w + \varepsilon_1 \\ \iota\alpha_2 + w + \varepsilon_2 \\ \cdot \\ \cdot \\ \cdot \\ \iota\alpha_N + w + \varepsilon_n \end{bmatrix}
$$

(where y_i is the vector of observations of the dependent variable of country i, N the number of countries, ι a vector of one's for each industry, k the vector of technical coefficients, w the vector of sector specific random effects and ε_j the vector of ε_{ij}'s).

The estimates of the total residual variance $(\sigma_\alpha^2 + \sigma_w^2 + \sigma^2)$ are reported in Table 2.3 and 2.4. We show below the estimates of the three components, their total and the variance of the dependent variable (d.v.) corresponding to the use of the Japanese technical coefficients.

	Exports		Imports		Net Exports	
	stock	flow	stock	flow	stock	flow
$\hat{\sigma}_\alpha^2$	0.52	0.48	0.31	0.30	0.09	0.08
$\hat{\sigma}_w^2$	0.51	0.63	0.24	0.26	0.02	0.03
$\hat{\sigma}^2$	3.00	3.07	1.08	1.10	0.20	0.21
total	4.03	4.18	1.63	1.66	0.31	0.32
d.v.	5.63	5.63	1.99	1.99	0.45	0.45

---

[1]/ Another interpretation of (I) is obtained by assuming that the α_j's are not random effects, but rather unknown parameters to be estimated. If in addition it is assumed that the variance of the sector specific random effect is equal to 0, so that w drops out, (I) can be estimated by ordinary least-squares (OLS) after dropping the column of ι's in the matrix of explanatory variables and the parameter d.

The variance of the sector specific effect is relatively small in all the cases, which is not surprising since there is a sector specific explanatory variable in the equation. The variance of the country specific effect [1] is also relatively small, while the general effect clearly dominates the variance of the residuals. All in all, the results of the present study seem remarkably robust with respect to the hypotheses on the disturbances in the various procedures.

Projections of the β coefficients

Using the 1979 endowments (GDICAP79 and HMIND79), and the 1971 second-stage estimated equations, we can derive two sets of projected values of the 1979 β coefficients. These procedures are defined in Section 2.5; they are illustrated by the use of an example in the following.

The 1971 second-stage estimated equation for exports, using the U.S. stock measure of capital intensity, is shown in (II). Now, the first set of projected 1979 β coefficients, denoted by $\hat{\beta}_{79/1}$ and called the projected "fitted" 1979 β coefficients, can be derived using (III). In turn, the second set of coefficients, denoted by $\beta_{79/1}$ and called the projected "estimated" 1979 β coefficients, can be derived using (IV).

Next, we compare $\hat{\beta}_{79/1}$ with the "fitted" 1979 β coefficients ($\hat{\beta}_{79}$) obtained as the fitted values of the 1979 second stage regression (V), and compare $\beta_{79/1}$ with the "observed" 1979 β coefficients (β_{79}) which are the first-stage estimated β coefficients for 1979.

(II) $\beta_{71} = -1.35 + 1.70 \text{ GDICAP71} + 0.33 \text{ HMIND71} + e_{71}$
        (where e_{71} denotes the estimated 1971 residuals)

(III) $\hat{\beta}_{79/1} = -1.35 + 1.70 \text{ (GDICAP79} - \text{GDICAP79} + \text{GDICAP71)}$
        $+ 0.33 \text{ (HMIND79} - \text{HMIND79} + \text{HMIND71)}$

---

[1] Under the estimation of (I) by OLS in one-pass, the residual variance is exactly equal to $\sigma_w + \sigma_\alpha$ since the σ_α residual variance is absorbed in the variance explained by the regression thanks to the estimation of the α_j coefficients.

(where a bar over a variable denotes the sample average) $\underline{1/}$

(IV) $\hat{\beta}_{79/1} = \hat{\beta}_{79/1} + e_{71}$.

(V) $\beta_{79} = -1.58 + 1.66 \text{ GDICAP79} + 0.30 \text{ HMIND79}.$

Note that $\beta_{79/1} = \hat{\beta}_{79/1} + e_{71}$, while $\beta_{79} = \hat{\beta}_{79} + e_{79}$. The rationale for adding the 1971 residuals e_{71} to $\beta_{79/1}$ in order to define $\beta_{79/1}$ and compare it with β_{79} is that β_{79} incorporates a random term e_{79} which can be approximated by its 1971 equivalent. $\underline{2/}$ In other words, we expect e_{79} and e_{71} to be strongly correlated, for if a country deviates much from the 1971 regression line it is likely to deviate in a similar way in 1979. This is because the deviations are due to structural characteristics that are not likely to change within the short period covered. In fact, all the correlations between the 1979 and the 1971 residuals are strong and their significance levels are high.

$\underline{1/}$ Adding the mean of each endowment variable in 1971 and subtracting the corresponding 1979 mean adjusts the constant term of (III) and results in projected coefficients with an average value approximately the same as that of the 1979 coefficients.

$\underline{2/}$ Statistically, the quality of the approximation of β_{79} by $\beta_{79/1}$ relies also on the absence of correlation between $\beta_{79/1}$ and e_{71} , since by properties of OLS, β_{79} is also uncorrelated with e_{71} . The correlation coefficients between $\beta_{79/1}$ and e_{79} are all close to zero and do not differ significantly from zero at the 1 percent level.

Chapter 3

COMPARATIVE ADVANTAGE IN A MULTI-PRODUCT
AND MULTI-FACTOR MODEL OF MULTILATERAL TRADE

3.1 A Multilateral Model of Comparative Advantage

In Chapter 2, the pattern of comparative advantage was analyzed by the use
of a two-stage procedure. In the first stage of estimation, indices of
comparative advantage vis-a-vis the rest of the world, calculated for
individual industries, were regressed on measures of physical and capital
intensity for each of 38 major exporters of manufactured goods. In the
second stage, the regression coefficients thus obtained, indicating the
relative capital intensity of the trade structure of the individual
countries, were regressed on the physical and human capital endowments of
the countries concerned in a cross-section framework.

In transposing results obtained in "commodity space" into "country space,"
the method applied provided a test of the Heckscher-Ohlin theory by
introducing factor endowments along with factor intensities in the process
of estimation. An estimation technique combining the two stages in a "one
pass" procedure was also utilized.

In Chapter 2, trade in particular industries of the individual countries
with the rest of the world was the unit of observation. This chapter
extends the investigation to a multi-country context in examining the
determinants of the network of trade among 38 principal exporters of
manufactured goods; i.e. it replaces a vector by a matrix of trade. This
involves gauging the effects of relative factor endowments on the factor
intensity of bilateral trade flows, defined in terms of net exports, in
the framework of a multilateral model.

As in the preceding chapter, three factors of productions are introduced
in the analysis: physical capital, human capital, and unskilled labor.

Factor intensities are expressed in terms of physical capital per worker
and human capital per worker, with calculations made using aggregated as
well as disaggregated measures of capital intensity. Factor endowments
are defined in a comparable manner, in terms of the stock of physical
capital and the stock of human capital. The investigation uses U.S. data
and covers 167 industries as beforehand.

Section 3.2 describes the methodology of estimation. Sections 3.3 and
3.4, respectively, report the results for the entire country group and for
individual country groups, respectively.

3.2 The Methodology of Estimation

The methodology applied involves two-stage as well as one-pass
estimation. These will be taken up in turn. In both cases, aggregated
capital intensities will be introduced first, followed by their
disaggregation into physical and human capital.

Two-Stage Estimation

In the first stage of estimation, normalized values of net bilateral
exports are regressed on capital-labor ratios; in the second, the
resulting regression coefficients for bilateral trade are regressed on
relative country endowment variables. The two stages of estimation are
expressed in (3.1) and (3.2) for the case when physical and human capital
intensities are aggregated and in (3.3) and (3.4) for the case when they
are separately introduced.

Aggregated Capital Intensities

$$NNX_{jki} = \alpha_{jk} + \beta_{jk}^{c} \ln c_i + u_{jki} \tag{3.1}$$

$$\beta_{jk}^{c} = a^c + b^c \ln \frac{G_j}{G_k} + d^c \ln \frac{H_j}{H_k} + v_{jk}^{c} \tag{3.2}$$

Disaggregated Capital Intensities

$$NNX_{jki} = \alpha_{jk} + \beta_{jk}^{p} \ln p_i + \beta_{jk}^{h} \ln h_i + u_{jki} \tag{3.3}$$

$$\text{(a)} \quad \beta_{jk}^{p} = a^{p} + b^{p}\ln\frac{G_{j}}{G_{k}} + v_{jk}^{p} \qquad\qquad (3.4)$$

$$\text{(b)} \quad \beta_{jk}^{h} = a^{h} + b^{h}\ln\frac{H_{j}}{H_{k}} + v_{jk}^{h}$$

In the equations, NNX stands for normalized net exports [1]; c refers to total (aggregate) capital intensity; p and h denote physical and human capital intensities, respectively; and G and H are the physical and human capital endowment variables. In turn, j (1...38) and k(1...37) are the country subscripts and i(1....167) the industry subscripts.

Since $NNX_{jki} = -NNX_{kji}$, in the model incorporating trade among all the countries under consideration there are potentially 703 $(\frac{jk}{2})$ equations pertaining to bilateral trade between pairs of countries in the first stage of estimation; in each equation there are potentially 167 observations. In fact, there are fewer numbers of equations and of non-zero observations, because of the lack of·trade flows between certain pairs of countries in some or all industries. Altogether 639 first-stage equations have been estimated with 67,989 observations as compared to a potential number of 117,401; correspondingly, there are 639 observations in estimating the second-stage equation.

(3.1) and (3.3) modify the equational forms used in Chapter 2 as the data now pertain to bilateral trade rather than to the trade of each country with the rest of the world. Regression coefficients β_{jk}^{c} in (3.1) and β_{jk}^{p} and β_{jk}^{h} in (3.3) thus show the estimated relationship between the pattern of net exports between countries j and k and the relative capital intensities of the individual industries.

In (3.2) and (3.4), intercountry differences in physical and human capital endowments are introduced to explain the pattern of the β -coefficients

---

[1] Normalization has been done by dividing the net exports of each industry between countries j and k ($X_{jki} - M_{jki}$) by the sum f these exports and imports ($X_{jki} + M_{jki}$). While normalization by the use of production data would have been preferable, such data are not available.

estimated in (3.1) and (3.3), respectively; in (3.4) this involves linking the physical capital intensity of bilateral trade to relative physical capital endowments and the human capital intensity of bilateral trade to relative human capital endowments. [1]/ The hypothesis is tested that countries which are relatively capital abundant will tend to export relatively capital-intensive products in bilateral trade.

We have experimented with two alternative definitions of relative capital endowments. One alternative, shown in (3.2) and (3.4), involves using the ratio of capital endowments in countries j and k, expressed in logarithmic terms; this is equivalent to using differences in logs. Another alternative involves using absolute differences in factor endowments $(G_j - G_k)$ and $(H_j - H_k)$ instead.

In most instances, the choice between the two alternatives has not affected the statistical significance of the regression coefficients. This indicates the robustness of the results to the specifications used as regards relative capital endowments. In the equations where this was not the case, the absolute difference form has generally worked better. Both sets of results are reported in the tables.

Ordinary least squares have been used in estimating (3.1) and (3.3). In order to adjust for heteroscedasticity, weighted least squares have been used in estimating (3.2) and generalized least squares in estimating (3.4). In the latter case, (3.4a) and (3.4b) have been simultaneously estimated.

One-pass Estimation

One-pass estimation combines the two stages of estimation, involving the use of interaction terms that relate capital intensities to capital endowments. Combining (3.1) and (3.2) yields (3.5) while combining (3.3)

---

[1]/ An attempt has been made to introduce cross-terms in equation (3.4) by adding $\ln H_j / H_k$ in (3.4a) and $\ln G_j / G_k$ in (3.4b). Due to the high multi-collinearity of the factor endowment variables, statistically significant results have not been obtained.

and (3.4) yields (3.6).

$$NNX_{jki} = \alpha_{jk} + a^c lnc_i + b^c ln \frac{G_j}{G_k} lnc_i + d^c ln \frac{H_j}{H_k} lnc_i + \varepsilon_{jki} \qquad (3.5)$$

where $\varepsilon_{jki} = v_{jk}^c \, lnc_i + u_{jki}$

$$NNX_{jki} = \alpha_{jk} + a^p lnp_i + a^h lnh_i + b^p ln \frac{G_j}{G_k} lnp_i + \qquad (3.6)$$

$$+ b^h ln \frac{H_j}{H_k} lnh_i + \varepsilon_{jki} \; ,$$

where $\varepsilon_{jki} = v_{jk}^p \, lnp_i + v_{jk}^h lnh_i + u_{jki}$

Comparisons of (3.2) and (3.5) and of (3.4) and (3.6) show that one can interpret the coefficients of lnc_i, lnp_i, and lnh_i in one-pass estimation as the constants of the second stage equation, and the coefficients of $lnG_j/G_k \, lnc_i$ and $lnH_j/H_k \, lnc_i$, as well as those of $lnG_j/G_k \, lnp_i$ and $lnH_j/H_k \, lnh_i$, as the coefficients of lnG_j/G_k and lnH_j/H_k in the second-stage equation. Under certain assumptions, the two sets of estimated coefficients will have equal values (Amemiya, 1978); however, their levels of statistical significance will differ, owing to differences in the number of observations.

(3.5) and (3.6) are expressed in linear terms. Another alternative involves utilizing a non-linear function as in (3.7) where γz_{jki} stands for the variables included in the model to be estimated; i.e. the right-hand side of (3.5) and (3.6) with the exclusion of the error term. This has been derived from the logistic function $y = 1/(1 + exp - t)$, where $0 \le y \le 1$,

$$NNX_{jki} = \frac{1 - exp - (\gamma\,z_{jki})}{1 + exp - (\gamma\,z_{jki})} + \varepsilon_{jki} \qquad (3.7)$$

utilizing the transformation $x - 2y - 1$. Thus,

$$-1 \le x = [2//(1 + exp - t)] - 1 - (1 - exp - t)/(1 + exp - t) \le 1$$

Estimation by non-linear least squares has the advantage of limiting the predicted values of the dependent variable to the range (-1, +1), which is

the range of the actual values of this variable. Also, it is not
necessary to include the country specific interaction term, α_{jk}, the
estimation of which would be costly and difficult as there are 639 such
terms. Given the advantages of non-linear least squares, and the
existence of considerable similarities between two sets of estimates, the
results obtained by ordinary least squares are not reported in the tables:
the estimates are available from the authors.

3.3   Empirical Results for the Entire Group of Countries

Tables 3.1 and 3.2, respectively, report the estimates made by the use of
the two-stage and the one-pass procedures for trade among all the
countries included in the investigation. The tables show estimates
obtained by using aggregated and disaggregated capital intensity
variables; stock and flow measures of capital; and relative capital
endowment variables expressed in terms of ratios and absolute differences.

In the estimated equations, the regression coefficients of the relative
capital endowment variables have the expected sign and, with one
exception, are statistically significant at the one percent level. The
sole exception is the human capital endowment variable in the case when
capital intensities are aggregated, relative capital endowments are
expressed in a ratio form, and the stock measure or capital intensity is
used.

The constants of the equations are statistically significant in all cases
when capital intensities are aggregated. This result has also obtained in
estimation by the use of the disaggregated form of capital intensity for
the constants pertaining to human, but not to physical, capital.
It further appears that the explanatory power of the regression equations
is greater in the event when capital intensities are aggregated rather
than disaggregated. Thus, the (adjusted) coefficient of determination is
in the 0.60-0.62 range in the first case and in the 0.42-0.48 range in the
second. At the same time, the adjusted R^2s are practically the same,
irrespective of whether the stock or the flow measure of capital intensity
is used when capital is aggregated while the use of the flow measures
gives a higher R^2 if capital is disaggregated. Finally, the coefficient

Table 3.1

Explanation of Intercountry Differences in the Pattern of Specialization in Manufactured Goods
in the Multilateral Framework: Trade Among All Countries a/
(WLS and GLS estimates of two-stage model, with t-values in parenthesis)

Definition of Intercountry Differences in Capital Endowment	Stock Flow	a^c	a^p	a^h	b^c	d^c	b^p	b^h	$\bar{R}^2$	N
ratio ^{b}	S	0.065 (3.85)			0.134 (11.52)	0.017 (0.96)			0.6044	639
	F	0.058 (3.37)			0.126 (10.51)	0.054 (2.89)			0.6015	639
difference ^{c}	S	0.052 (3.08)			0.608 (11.71)	0.079 (5.05)			0.6186	639
	F	0.041 (2.37)			0.609 (11.45)	0.105 (6.57)			0.6224	639
ratio ^{b}	S		0.000 (0.00)	0.137 (13.66)			0.064 (8.65)	0.069 (6.16)	0.4167	1264
	F		0.002 (0.13)	0.136 (12.56)			0.088 (10.64)	0.077 (6.49)	0.4817	1264
difference ^{c}	S		0.008 (0.60)	0.132 (13.77)			0.298 (7.79)	0.084 (7.67)	0.4191	1264
	F		0.015 (0.97)	0.129 (12.48)			0.398 (9.34)	0.097 (8.44)	0.4775	1264

(a) For explanation of symbols, see text. Levels of statistical significance of 1, 5 and 10 percent, derived in two-tail tests, are denoted by **, *, and W, respectively.

(b) $\ln \frac{G_j}{G_k}$, $\ln \frac{H_j}{H_k}$;   (c) $(G_j - G_k)$, $(H_j - H_k)$

Table 3.2

Explanation of Intercountry Differences in the Pattern of Specialization in Manufactured Goods in the Multilateral Framework: Trade Among All Countries a/
(logistic estimates of the one-pass model, with t-values in parenthesis)

Definition of Intercountry Differences in Capital Endowment	Stock Flow	a^c	a^p	a^h	b^c	d^c	b^p	b^h	s^2	N
ratio b	S	0.027 (8.48)			0.135 (46.71)	0.027 (6.42)			0.1565	67989
	F	0.028 (8.70)			0.136 (46.72)	0.029 (6.62)			0.1569	67989
difference c	S	0.063 (18.87)			0.513 (42.75)	0.016 (4.82)			0.1613	67989
	F	0.065 (18.99)			0.517 (42.38)	0.017 (4.94)			0.1617	67989
ratio b	S		-0.109 (9.73)	0.116 (13.74)			0.209 (47.91)	0.033 (6.83)	0.1552	67989
	F		-0.149 (11.73)	0.141 (16.26)			0.215 (45.94)	0.038 (7.86)	0.1559	67989
difference c	S		-0.074 (6.64)	0.132 (15.75)			0.782 (43.44)	0.022 (5.69)	0.1601	67989
	F		-0.110 (8.78)	0.156 (18.27)			0.814 (41.74)	0.024 (6.26)	0.1607	67989

(a) For explanation of symbols, see text.

(b) $\ln \frac{G_j}{G_k}$, $\ln \frac{H_j}{H_k}$;   (c) (G_j-G_k), (H_j-H_k)

of determination is not affected by the choice of the ratio and the difference form of relative capital endowments.

One-pass estimation by non-linear least squares does not permit deriving the coefficient of determination. But, all the regression coefficients are statistically significant at the 1 percent level in every equation, irrespective of the specifications applied, with the t-values ranging between 4.8 and 46.8. At the same time, the constant terms pertaining to the physical capital endowment variable that were not significant statistically under two-stage estimation are statistically significant and have a negative sign under one-pass estimation.

In demonstrating that the factor intensity of bilateral trade in manufactured goods can be explained in terms of relative factor endowments, the empirical results of the paper provide support to the Heckscher-Ohlin theory of comparative advantage. This conclusion obtains under several alternative specifications and utilizing a two-stage was well as a one-pass estimation procedure, with the latter procedure generally providing stronger results in terms of the statistical significance of the regression coefficients.

The estimates made under alternative specifications also indicate the appropriateness of aggregating physical and human capital. This result reinforces that obtained in Chapter 2 while contrasting with the results of several authors referred to in that chapter.

3.4 Empirical Results for Individual Groups of Countries

Estimates have further been made for trade among the developed countries, trade between developed and developing countries, trade among developing countries, and trade among European countries. Tables 3.3 to 3.6 report the estimates obtained by the use of the two-stage procedure in the three cases.

The estimates reported in Table 3.3 for trade among developed countries generally confirm the results obtained for trade among all the countries under consideration. The explanatory power of the two sets of regressions is very similar, except that the use of the flow measure of capital intensity now gives lower coefficients of determination if capital is disaggregated.

In the estimates made for trade among developed countries, the regression coefficients of the relative capital endowment variables are significant at the 1 percent level in all cases when capital intensities are aggregated. The same result obtains in cases when capital intensity is introduced in a disaggregated form, except that the physical capital-endowment variable is not statistically significant at even the 10 percent level when the flow measure of capital intensity is used. At the same time, the levels of significance of the constants of the regression equations vary, depending on the specifications used.

The coefficients of determination are particularly high in the case of estimates for trade between developed and developing countries (Table 3.4); they are around 0.75 in cases when capital intensities are aggregated and 0.65 when capital intensities are disaggregated, with little variation shown in the estimates under alternative specifications. The high degree of explanatory power of the regressions estimated for trade between developed and developing countries may be explained by the exclusion of trade among developing countries, where intercountry differences in factor endowments are less important and have low explanatory power as noted below.

In estimates made for trade between developed and developing countries, the regression coefficients of the physical capital endowment variable are statistically significant at the 1 percent level in all the equations. In turn, the level of significance of the human capital endowment variable depends on whether relative capital endowments are introduced in ratio or in a difference form. While the regression coefficients are significant at the 5 percent or, at least at the 10 percent, level in the latter case, they are not statistically significant in the former. Finally, the statistical significance of the constants of the regression equations again varies depending on the specifications used.

The coefficients of determination do not reach 0.1, and few of the

Table 3.3

Explanation of Intercountry Differences in the Pattern of Specialization in Manufactured Goods in the Multilateral Framework: Trade Among Developed Countries [a] (WLS and GLS estimates of two-stage model, with t-values in parenthesis)

Definition of Intercountry Differences in Capital Endowment	Stock Flow	a^c	a^p	a^h	b^c	d^c	b^p	b^h	$\bar{R}^2$	N
ratio [b]	S	0.025 (1.58)			0.197 (5.88)	0.249 (8.28)			0.6028	153
	F	0.044 (2.69)			0.140 (4.10)	0.282 (9.28)			0.6058	153
difference [c]	S	0.019 (1.20)			0.478 (6.46)	0.151 (9.61)			0.6346	153
	F	0.036 (2.27)			0.360 (4.81)	0.167 (10.53)			0.6399	153
ratio [b]	S		-0.016 (1.22)	0.070 (7.94)			0.151 (5.54)	0.148 (6.84)	0.4240	306
	F		0.039 (2.36)	0.069 (7.30)			0.045 (1.29)	0.136 (5.75)	0.3451	306
difference [c]	S		-0.011 (0.86)	0.067 (7.83)			0.318 (5.04)	0.090 (7.66)	0.4359	306
	F		0.039 (2.42)	0.067 (7.18)			0.100 (1.25)	0.083 (6.54)	0.3654	306

(a) For explanation of symbols, see text.

(b) $\ln \frac{G}{G_k}$, $\ln \frac{H}{H_k}$; (c) $(G_j - G_k)$, $(H_j - H_k)$

Table 3.4

Explanation of Intercountry Differences in the Pattern of Specialization in Manufactured Goods in the Multilateral Framework: Trade Between Developed and Developing Countries a/

(WLS and GLS estimates of two-stage model, with t-values in parenthesis)

Definition of Intercountry Differences in Capital Endowment	Stock Flow	a^c	a^p	a^h	b^c	d^c	b^p	b^h	$\bar{R}^2$	N
ratio b	S	0.109 (3.33)			0.129 (8.07)	-0.018 (0.87)			0.7577	352
	F	0.099 (2.80)			0.131 (7.56)	0.005 (0.21)			0.7427	352
difference c	S	0.062 (1.77)			0.667 (8.24)	0.034 (1.78)			0.7643	352
	F	0.058 (1.53)			0.678 (7.74)	0.052 (2.52)			0.7491	352
ratio b	S		-0.014 (0.70)	0.239 (14.38)			0.066 (7.53)	0.004 (0.26)	0.6512	704
	F		0.012 (0.50)	0.249 (14.28)			0.073 (7.01)	0.007 (0.41)	0.6494	704
difference c	S		0.001 (0.05)	0.216 (14.05)			0.301 (6.19)	0.033 (2.20)	0.6449	704
	F		0.027 (1.05)	0.229 (14.25)			0.339 (5.85)	0.033 (2.06)	0.6441	704

(a) For explanation of symbols, see text.

(b) $\ln \frac{G_j}{G_k}$, $\ln \frac{H_j}{H_k}$;   (c) $(G_j - G_k)$, $(H_j - H_k)$

regression coefficients are statistically significant, in the estimates made for trade among developing countries (Table 3.5). And, in the cases when the physical capital endowment variable is statistically significant at the 5 percent level, the human capital endowment variable is not significant.

It would appear, then, that the Heckscher–Ohlin theory, which well explains trade in manufactured goods among all the principal countries exporting these commodities, among developed countries, as well as between developed and developing countries, fails to provide an adequate explanation for trade in manufactured goods among the developing countries. While this, negative, result requires further study, some possible explanations may be put forward.

A contributing factor has been the poor quality of the data. To begin with, trade data for the developing countries involve considerable error, in particular as far as their geographical breakdown is concerned. Also, the use of U.S. input coefficients will introduce greater error possibilities for developing than for developed countries. Finally, estimates of factor endowments for developing countries, based on cumulated investment data that are themselves subject to uncertainty, are open to greater errors than the comparable estimates for developed countries.

An additional consideration is that the variability of industrial protection is substantially greater in developing than in developed countries. Apart from the results of effective protection studies, this conclusion is confirmed by calculations reported in Chapter 2, where the extent of trade orientation was measured in terms of deviations of actual from predicted exports per head, the latter being derived from a cross-section regression equation incorporating per capita incomes, population, mineral exports, and distance as explanatory variables. The results show that the standard deviation of the residuals is three times higher for developing than for developed countries.

The idiosyncracies of the pattern of industrial protection in developing countries weaken the effects of differences in factor endowments on trade in manufactured goods among developing countries. A further distorting factor is the existence of preferential arrangements among developing countries, in particular, in Latin America. In fact, there is evidence that such arrangements have led to considerable deviations from the pattern of comparative advantage in trade among the LAFTA countries (Krueger, 1983, ch. 6).

The coefficients of determination are among the highest in the case of estimates for trade among European countries (Table 3.6); they are 0.74 in cases when capital intensities are aggregated and 0.73 when they are disaggregated. Also, all the regression coefficients of the capital endowment variables are statistically significant at the 1 percent level. In most instances, the constant term is also significant at the 1 percent level. However, it changes sign when intercountry differences in capital endowment are expressed in a ratio form and the stock measure of capital is used.

3.5 Summary

The chapter has used a multilateral trade model to explain the pattern of bilateral trade in manufactured goods among major exporters of these products by reference to inter-industry differences in factor intensities and intercountry differences in factor endowments. This has been accomplished by utilizing a two-stage as well as a one-pass procedure. In the former case, standardized net exports are regressed on measures of capital intensity for each pair of countries and the regression coefficients thus obtained are regressed on relative capital intensity in a cross-section framework; in the latter case, the two stages of estimation are combined into one.

The results obtained for trade among the 38 principal exporters of manufactured goods provide support to the Heckscher-Ohlin theory: they show that countries which are relatively abundant in physical and in human capital tend to export relatively physical and human capital intensive products in bilateral trade. This conclusion does not depend on the choice of the estimation procedure or on the specifications utilized. Thus, it is unaffected by the use of a two-stage or one-pass procedure,

Table 3.5

Explanation of Intercountry Differences in the Pattern of Specialization in Manufactured Goods in the Multilateral Framework: Trade Among Developing Countries a/

(WLS and OLS estimates of two-stage model, with t-values in parenthesis)

Definition of Intercountry Differences in Capital Endowment	Stock Flow	a^c	a^p	a^h	b^c	d^c	b^p	b^h	$\bar{R}^2$	N
ratio b	S	0.049 (0.70)			0.112 (1.74)	-0.033 (0.57)			0.0874	134
	F	0.022 (0.33)			0.081 (1.30)	0.034 (0.59)			0.0557	134
difference c	S	0.089 (1.37)			0.863 (0.94)	0.005 (0.06)			0.0732	134
	F	0.030 (0.47)			1.091 (1.25)	0.083 (0.92)			0.0593	134
ratio b	S		0.039 (0.62)	0.082 (2.41)			0.036 (0.64)	-0.019 (0.44)	0.0321	254
	F		0.001 (0.01)	0.064 (1.88)			0.127 (2.45)	-0.012 (0.38)	0.0877	254
difference c	S		0.123 (2.08)	0.078 (2.35)			-0.895 (-1.13)	-0.015 (0.21)	0.0346	254
	F		0.029 (0.44)	0.060 (1.78)			1.685 (2.12)	0.007 (0.11)	0.0826	254

(a) For explanation of symbols, see text.

(b) $\ln \dfrac{G_j}{G_k}$, $\ln \dfrac{H_j}{H_k}$;   (c) $(G_j - G_k)$, $(H_j - H_k)$

Table 3.6

Explanation of Intercountry Differences in the Pattern of Specialization
in Manufactured Goods in the Multilateral Framework: Trade among European Countries a/
(WLS and OLS estimates of two-stage model, with t-values in parenthesis)

Definition of Intercountry Differences in Capital Endowment	Stock	a^c	a^p	a^l	b^c	d^c	b^e	b^h	$\bar{R}^2$
ratio b	S	0.260 (14.21)	–	–	0.144 (22.56)	0.092 (7.72)	–	–	0.7415
	F	0.290 (15.37)	–	–	0.145 (22.26)	0.094 (7.77)	–	–	0.7432
difference c	S	0.300 (16.31)	–	–	0.203 (10.33)	0.237 (22.71)	–	–	0.7312
	F	0.328 (17.31)	–	–	0.201 (10.04)	0.242 (22.72)	–	–	0.7321
ratio b	S	–	-0.051 (2.77)	0.245 (14.71)	–	–	0.219 (23.13)	0.118 (8.82)	0.7413
	F	–	0.045 (2.05)	0.228 (13.74)	–	–	0.234 (22.50)	0.115 (8.61)	0.7419
difference c	S	–	0.029 (1.58)	0.220 (13.24)	–	–	0.321 (11.12)	0.275 (23.03)	0.7302
	F	–	0.131 (5.94)	0.204 (12.55)	–	–	0.326 (10.23)	0.275 (23.26)	0.7311

(a) For explanation of results, see text.

(b) $\ln \frac{G_j}{G_k}$, $\ln \frac{H_j}{H_k}$; (c) $(G_j - G_k)$, $(H_j - H_k)$

estimation by linear or non-linear equations, the use of aggregated or disaggregated capital intensity, the measurement of capital intensity in stock or in flow terms, and the choice of the ratio or the difference form in defining relative capital endowments.

The conclusion is reconfirmed by estimates made for trade among developed countries, between developed and developing countries, and among European countries.   However, the Heckscher-Ohlin theory has not been successfully tested in regard to trade among developing countries.   In the latter case, data   limitations,   the   variability   of   industrial   protection,   and preferential arrangements appear to have affected the results.

These results do not infirm, however, the conclusions reached in Chapter 2, according to which the export composition of the developing countries in manufactured products changes in a predictable fashion as they accumulate physical and human capital.   The result of the multilateral model, then, can be interpreted in terms of the stages approach to international specialization that permits one to trace prospective changes in the export composition of the developing countries.

Part II

**THE DETERMINANTS OF INTRA-INDUSTRY TRADE
IN MANUFACTURED GOODS**

Chapter 4

CONCEPTUAL AND MEASUREMENT ISSUES

4.1 The Meaning and Measurement of Intra-Industry Trade

Since the time the concept of intra-industry -- as compared to inter-industry -- trade was first introduced (Balassa, 1966), a vast literature has developed on the subject. Early efforts concentrated on the measurement of the extent of intra-industry specialization. [1] Subsequently, several contributions were made to the theory of intra-industry trade and empirical investigations were also undertaken to examine the determinants of intra-industry specialisation. [2]

This study tests alternative hypotheses as to the factors affecting the extent of intra-industry trade, defined as the share of this trade in total trade. The investigation is limited to trade in manufactured goods where product differentiation predominates while trade in primary commodities occurs largely in standardized products. Seasonal and border trade apart, intra-industry specialization is not expected to take place in standardized commodities. [3]

The investigation covers 38 countries whose manufactured exports exceeded $300 million, and accounted for at least 18 percent of their total merchandise exports, in 1979. Eighteen countries with per capita incomes

---

[1] The expressions "intra-industry specialisation" and "intra-industry trade" will be used interchangeably in this study.

[2] For references, see below.

[3] However, Brander (1981) considers the case of intra-industry trade in standardized commodities under conditions of Cournot-type duopoly.

of \$2254 or higher in 1973, 1/ have been included in the developed, and
twenty countries with per capita incomes of \$2031 or lower in 1973 2/ in
the developing country group (Table 1.1). 3/

The investigation covers 167 industry categories in the manufacturing
sector as defined by the United States Standard Industrial Classification
(SIC), with the exclusion of natural resource products whose manufacture
is importantly affected by the availability of natural resources in a
particular country. 4/ The classification scheme, shown in Table 1.2, has
been established by merging 4-digit SIC categories in cases when the
economic characteristics of particular products have been judged to be
very similar. The use of an economically meaningful classification scheme
is of importance, so as to identify 'genuine' as compared to spurious
intra-industry trade -- which latter is an artifact of the classification
scheme employed. The individual industry categories have further been

----

1/   In order of per capita GNP, the countries in question are Switzerland,
     United States, Sweden, Denmark, Germany, Australia, Canada, Norway,
     France, Belgium, Netherlands, Japan, Finland, Austria, United Kingdom,
     Israel, Italy, and Ireland.

2/   In order of their per capita incomes, they are Spain, Singapore,
     Greece, Argentina, Hong Kong, Portugal, Yugoslavia, Mexico, Brazil,
     Taiwan, Malaysia, Tunisia, Korea, Morocco, Turkey, Egypt, Thailand,
     Philippines, India, and Pakistan.

3/   Among empirical studies of the intercountry determinants of intra-
     industry trade, Havrylyshyn and Civan (1983) included countries such
     as Algeria, the Central African Republic, Nigeria, and Sudan, whose
     exports of manufactured goods accounted for less than one percent of
     total. In turn, Bergstrand (1983), Clair, Gaussens, and Phan (1984),
     and Loertscher and Wolter (1980) limited the investigation to trade
     among developed countries. All other empirical studies of intra-
     industry trade, referred to below, examined the interindustry
     determinants of this trade.

4/   The investigation excludes foods and beverages (SIC 20), tobacco (SIC
     21), non-ferrous metals (SIC 333), as well as several 4-digit
     categories covering textile waste, preserved wood, saw mill products,
     prefabricated wood, veneer and plywood, wood pulp, dyeing and tanning
     extracts, fertilizers, adhesives and gelatin, carbon black, petroleum
     refining and products, asbestos and asphalt products, cement and
     concrete, lime, gypsum products, cut stone products, and lapidary
     work. It also excludes ordnance (SIC 19), for which comparable trade
     data are not available.

matched against the 3- and 4-digit categories of the United Nations Standard International Trade Classification (SITC). 1/

Sections 4.2 and 4.3, respectively, describe the principal hypotheses introduced by various authors regarding the country and the industry characteristics affecting intra-industry trade. Section 4.4 provides a short outline of the remaining chapters of Part II.

4.2 Country Characteristics Affecting Intra-Industry Trade

A variety of hypotheses have been put forward as to the effects of country characteristics on intra-industry trade. In examining trade in differentiated products, Linder advanced the proposition that "the more similar the demand structures of two countries, the more intensive, potentially, is the trade between these two countries" (1961, p. 94). He further claimed that while "a whole array of forces influences the demand structure of a country...the level of average income is the most important single factor and that it has, in fact, a dominating influence on the structure of demand, [hence] similarity of average income levels could be used as an index of similarity of demand structures" (Ibid.). The converse of this proposition is that "per capita income differences are a

---

1/ Among other empirical studies of intra-industry trade, Havrylyshyn and Civan (1983) and Pagoulatos and Sorensen (1975) used 102 3-digit SITC categories; Loertscher and Wolter selected 59 such categories because of a lack of sufficient reliable export data for others (1980, p. 285n); Caves chose 84 3-digit SITC categories which could be matched with 4-digit SIC categories (1981, p. 206); Toh utilized 112 4-digit SIC categories for which comparable trade data could be "derived from aggregating comparable and not too many SITC numbers in order to keep the extent of statistical aggregation bias to the minimum" (1982, p. 288); Lundberg (1982) made calculations for the 77 manufacturing sectors of the International Standard Industrial Classification; Bergstrand (1983) used 3 digit categories within SITC class 7, and Clair, Gaussens, and Phan (1984) utilized 5-digit categories in SITC classes 5 and 7. None of these authors attempted to replace the statistical categories by more appropriate industry categories or to exclude natural-resource products. In turn, several of them introduced variables to evaluate the implications for the index of intra-industry trade of the heterogeneity of the statistical categories, which is not necessary if an economically meaningful system of classification is used.

potential obstacle to trade.... When per capita income differences reach a certain magnitude, trade can only take place in certain qualitatively homogeneous products" (Ibid., p. 98).

In utilizing a model where intra-industry trade occurs in differentiated manufactured goods produced under economies of scale, Helpman subsequently provided a proof of the proposition that, in the case when the home country has a lower (or equal) capital-labor ratio than the foreign country and factor prices are equalized, "if we reallocate the world's labor and capital stock in a way which increases the foreign country's capital-labor ratio and reduces the home country's capital-labor ratio without disturbing commodity prices and factor rewards, then the share of intra-industry trade...will decline" (1981, p. 325). Now, "since the higher the capital-labor ratio the higher is income per capita (in a cross country comparison), this raises the hypothesis that a country's share of bilateral intra-industry trade is negatively correlated with the absolute difference in bilateral incomes per capita" (Ibid., p. 337). Subsequently, Helpman and Krugman reformulated this proposition in stating that "on the average the more similar countries are in 'per' capita income, the larger the share of intra-industry trade in their bilateral trade volume" (1985, p. 173).

Helpman also provided a proof of the proposition that, in two countries that have the same capital-labor ratio, "a redistribution of resources which preserves each country's initial capital-labor ratio increases the volume of trade if it reduces the inequality in country size, and it reduces the volume of trade if it increases the inequality in country size. The volume of trade is largest when both countries are of equal size" (Ibid. p. 327). On the assumptions made, the entire increase in trade takes the form of intra-industry specialization. Correspondingly, one may hypothesize that the extent of intra-industry trade between any two countries will be negatively correlated with the difference in their size.

The two propositions were combined by Dixit and Norman who concluded that "if the two countries are of similar size, and have no clear comparative advantage across industries, then we will see the predominant pattern of

trade as one of intra-industry trade" (1980, p. 288). Comparative
advantage is defined in terms of differences in factor endowments, for
which per capita income differences may again be used as a proxy.

Linder further suggested that "the higher the per capita income, the
higher will be the degree of quality characterizing the demand structure
as a whole" (1961, p. 99), when higher product quality is embodied in
"more complex, elaborated, refined or luxurious" (Ibid.) products. As
these products tend to be differentiated, the extent of intra-industry
trade between any two countries is expected to be greater, the higher is
their average per capita income.

Finally, Lancaster showed that, owing to economies of scale, the
equilibrium number of differentiated manufactured products will be the
greater, the larger is the size of the market (1980, p. 158).
Correspondingly, it may be hypothesized that the extent of intra-industry
trade between any two countries will be positively correlated with their
average size.

We have considered various hypotheses linking the level of per capita
incomes and country size, and intercountry differences thereof, to the
extent of intra-industry trade. According to these hypotheses, the extent
of intra-industry trade between two countries is expected to be positively
correlated with their average per capita income and their average size and
negatively correlated with intercountry differences in their per capita
income and in their size.

In testing there hypotheses, per capita income will be measured by GNP per
head and country size by GNP. [1] But, rather than taking absolute values
of intercountry differences in per capita incomes and size, use has been
made of a relative inequality measure that takes values between 0 and 1.

1/ While the domestic consumption of manufactured goods would have been a
   more appropriate measure of the size of domestic market for these
   products, the necessary data are not available for some countries and
   are subject to considerable error in regard to others. At the same
   time, the consumption of manufactured goods and the gross national
   product are highly correlated.

This measure is superior to utilizing the absolute values of the
differences, which latter are affected by the magnitudes of the particular
country characteristics in the different countries. [1] The relative
inequality measure is shown in (4.1), where w refers to the ratio of a

(4.1)   INEQ = 1 + [(w) ln (w) + (1-w) ln (1-w)]/ln2

particular country characteristic in country j to the sum of this
characteristic in country j and partner country k.

The next question concerns the introduction of transportation costs. In
models of intra-industry trade, such as that of Krugman (1980),
transportation costs will reduce the volume of such trade. However, the
literature does not provide us with a presumption that intra-industry
trade will thereby be affected relatively more (or less) than inter-
industry trade. Such a presumption may be established if information
flows are introduced.

There is no need to provide information on the characteristics of
standardized (non-differentiated) products, such as copper metal, steel
ingots, and caustic soda, which have uniform specifications across the
world and hence their trade is determined largely by relative costs,
giving rise to inter-industry specialization. However, there is need for
information on the characteristics of differentiated products, such as
machinery, transport equipment, and consumer goods, which are subject to
intra-industry trade.

It can be assumed that the availability of information decreases, and its
cost increases, with distance. Correspondingly, it may be hypothesized
that the extent of intra-industry trade between any two countries will be
negatively correlated with the distance between them. Distance has been
measured in terms of miles between the centers of geographical gravity for

---

[1]   This measure is symmetrical with respect to country characteristics;
it is not affected by the unit of measurement; and it is a convex
function of w. It was first used by Bowden (1983).

each pair of countries. $\underline{1}/$

The existence of common borders will also contribute to information
flows. Furthermore, as Grubel and Lloyd suggested, in countries sharing a
common border, intra-industry trade may occur "in products which are
functionally homogeneous but differentiated by location" (1976, p. 5).
Thus, it may be hypothesized that the extent of intra-industry trade will
be greater between countries that share a common border than between
countries which do not have common borders. At the same time, the
separate introduction of distance and border variables permits testing the
hypothesis that common borders have economic significance for intra-
industry trade beyond that of distance. In the econometric investigation,
the existence of common borders has been represented by a dummy variable,
which takes the value of 1 when the two countries share a common border
and is 0 otherwise.

In a model incorporating specific capital and constant returns to scale,
Falvey found that the volume of intra-industry trade will vary inversely
with the level of tariffs and of trade restrictions in general (1981, p.
505). But, again, the question is if tariffs will affect intra-industry
trade relatively more than inter-industry trade. It has been suggested
that such would be the case in the event of trade liberalization in
general and economic integration in particular.

Thus, "once manufacturing industries have been established, the
elimination of protective measures on trade among developed countries does
not appear to reverse the effects these measures had on industrial
composition and the location of industry" (Balassa, 1977, p. 250). This
is because adjustment to reductions in trade barriers would occur largely
through rationalizing operations and changing the product composition of
individual industries, with national product differentiation contributing
to intra-industry trade (Balassa, 1967).

$\underline{1}/$ In measuring distance, adjustment has been made for the closure of the
Suez Canal in 1971.

It has further been shown that trade liberalization (Balassa, 1967) and economic integration in the European (Balassa, 1966, 1975) and the Latin American (Balassa, 1979) area were in fact accompanied by increases in the extent of intra-industry trade among the countries in question. In the present investigation, the hypotheses will be tested that the extent of intra-industry trade between any two countries is negatively correlated with the average level of their trade restrictions and positively correlated with participation in integration schemes.

Estimates of tariff levels are not available for a number of countries and the tariff equivalent of quantitative import restrictions is not known with any confidence for others. Correspondingly, the indicator of trade orientation, introduced in Chapter 2, has been used in the estimation.

For any pair of countries, the sum of their trade orientation index has been introduced in the estimating equations to test the hypothesis that the extent of intra-industry trade is positively correlated with trade orientation. In turn, dummy variables have been included to represent participation in the European Common Market (EEC), the European Free Trade Association (EFTA), and the Latin American Free Trade Area (LAFTA). [1]

Familiarity with each other's products may also contribute to intra-industry trade between particular countries. As common language breeds familiarity, it can be hypothesized that the existence of a common language will increase the extent of intra-industry trade between any two countries. This hypothesis will be tested in regard to English, French, Spanish, German, Portuguese, and Scandinavian languages by introducing a dummy variable for any pair of countries where the same language is used.

Table 4.1 provides a list of variables used to represent country characteristics affecting intra-industry trade that are the explanatory variables in the subsequent econometric investigation.

---

[1] For example, the EEC dummy is equal to 1 when both countries are members, and to 0 in all other cases.

Table 4.1

Definition of Variables [1/] Affecting Intra-Industry Trade between Two Countries (used as explanatory variables in the equations reported in Chapters 6 to 9)

Country characteristics

Common_characteristics [2/]

ln AY/P	(+):	natural logarithm of AY/P, the simple average of per capita incomes of the two countries (with per capita income measured by per capita GNP).
INEQ Y	(-):	measure of relative inequality between the per capita incomes of the two countries (as defined in section 4.2).
ln AY	(+):	natural logarithm of AY, the simple average of the sizes of the two countries (with size measured by GNP).
INEQ Y	(-):	measure of relative inequality between the GNP's of the two countries (as defined in equation 4.1).
ATO	(+):	sum of the trade orientation index of the two countries. The index is defined as the percentage deviation between observed and hypothetical capital exports, where hypothetical values are the fitted values derived from equation (2.6).
ln D	(-):	natural logarithm of the distance between the two countries, defined as mileage between their geographical centers.
BORDER	(+):	= 1 if the two countries have a common border, = 0 otherwise.

Specific_characteristics [2/]

EEC	(+):	= 1 if the two countries are members of the European Common Market, = 0 otherwise.
EFTA	(+):	= 1 if the two countries are members of the European Free Trade Association, = 0 otherwise.

LAFTA   (+): = 1 if the two countries are members of the
                                Latin American Free Trade Association, = 0
                                otherwise.

ENGLISH   (+): = 1 if the official language of the two
                                countries is English, = 0 otherwise.

FRENCH   (+): = 1 if the official language (or one of the
                                official languages) of two countries is
                                French, = 0 otherwise.

SPANISH   (+): = 1 if the official language of the two
                                countries is Spanish, = 0 otherwise.

PORT(UGUESE)   (+): = 1 if the official language of the two
                                countries is Portuguese, = 0 otherwise.

GERMAN   (+): = 1 if the official language (or one of
                                them) of the two countries is German, = 0
                                otherwise.

SCAND(INAVIAN)   (+): = 1 if one of the two countries belongs to
                                the Scandinavian cultural group (i.e.
                                Denmark, Sweden, Norway and Finland) = 0
                                otherwise.

Industry characterics
PD   (+): Hufbauer's (1970) coefficient of variation
                                of export unit values in a given industry,
                                as a measure of product differentiation.

MKT   (+): one of Caves' (1981) measure of product
                                differentiation defined as the share of
                                marketing, planning and support costs in
                                total costs in that industry.

ECSC   (-): Caves' (1981) measure of economies of scale
                                for a given industry, obtained by dividing
                                the ratio of the average size of shipments
                                of the largest plants in the industry
                                (accounting for approximately one-half of
                                industry shipments) to total industry
                                shipments, by the ratio of value added per
                                worker in the smaller plants (accounting
                                for the remaining half of industry
                                shipments) to value added per worker in the

larger plants.

IACR (-): Toh's (1982) internationally adjusted concentration ratio in a given industry, defined as the ratio of the share of the four largest firms in the industry output to the share of imports in the industry's output.

OAP (+): a measure of the extent of offshore assembly provisions, defined as the share of imports of the industry exempted from duties under offshore assembly provisions, to total imports of that industry.

Notes 1/ The signs in parentheses indicate the expected sign of the partial derivative of the extent of intra-industry trade with respect to that variable.

2/ Common characteristics pertain to all countries in the sample; specific characteristics apply to only some of them.

3/ All the data are for the U.S. industries.

4.3 Industry Characteristics Affecting Intra-Industry Trade

As far as industry characteristics are concerned, Linder (1961) and Dreze
(1960) were the first to emphasize the importance of product
differentiation in international trade. In the theoretical models of
Krugman (1979, 1980), Lancaster (1980) and Helpman (1981), product
differentiation is taken to be a precondition of intra-industry
specialization.

Hufbauer (1970) used the coefficient of variation of export unit values as
a measure of product differentiation on the assumption that an inverse
relationship exists between the degree of product standardization and the
dispersion of prices within each category. While Gray and Martin (1980)
criticized this procedure on the grounds that unit values do not
appropriately represent prices, at the 7-digit level of the SITC
classification scheme utilized by Hufbauer differences in unit values can
be assumed to largely reflect differences in product characteristics. At
any rate, for lack of price observations in the necessary detail, the
hedonic price indices suggested by Gray and Martin are not practicable.
Consequently, following Caves (1981) and Toh (1982), in the present study
use has been made of the Hufbauer measure of product differentiation.

Caves utilized Hufbauer's measure of product differentiation along with
other indicators arranged on a scale, reflecting the assumption that
'complexity' would favor international trade and 'information' would
discourage it. In descending order, following Hufbauer's proxy for
product differentiation, the variables are research and development costs
as a percentage of sales; selling costs as a percentage of total costs;
marketing, planning, and support costs as a percentage of total costs; and
advertising expenditures as a percentage of sales. After considerable
experimentation, only marketing expenditures have been introduced as an
additional measure of product differentiation in this study.

Theorists of intra-industry trade hold that economies of scale are a sine
qua non condition of intra-industry specialization; in the absence of
scale economies, all product varieties could be produced domestically and
no intra-industry trade would take place. Various measures were employed

as proxies for economies of scale in empirical investigations of intra-industry trade.   Hufbauer regressed value added per man on firm size, measured in terms of employment; Loertscher and Wolter (1980) used average value added per establishment; Caves (1981) divided minimum plant size by a measure of the cost disadvantages of small firms; and Lundberg (1982) utilized the share of labor force in firms having more than 500 workers for this purpose.

All these measures relate costs to plant size.   This is not the relevant measure, however, for economies of scale in industries producing differentiated products, characterized by horizontal and vertical specialization.   The former involves lessening product variety in individual plants while the latter entails producing parts, components, and accessories of a particular product in different plants. [1] Now, vertical and horizontal specialization may involve reducing -- rather than increasing -- plant size.

Correspondingly, the above measures of economies of scale will reflect the relative importance of product standardization and are expected to be negatively correlated with the extent of intra-industry trade.   In the present investigation, use has been made of Caves' measure. [2] This involves dividing the ratio of the average size of shipments of the largest plants in U.S. industry, accounting for approximately one-half of industry shipments, to total industry shipment, by the ratio of value added per worker in the smaller plants, again accounting for one-half of industry shipments, to value added per worker in the larger plants.

In turn, Toh (1982) suggested defining the length of the production run, associated with reductions in product variety, as the ratio of expenditures on new machinery to the capitalized value of the difference between the average wage and the unskilled wage.   However, this measure

---

[1]   These concepts were first introduced in Balassa, 1967.

[2]   Caves also expects a negative sign for this variable on the grounds that extensive scale economies would confine production to a few locations.   This notion again pertains to standardized rather than to differentiated products.

indicates the relative physical capital intensity of the production process rather than the length of the production run. At any rate, the use of this variable has not given statistically significant results in the present investigation and it has been excluded from the estimating equations reported in the tables.

Product standardization is further related to the extent of industrial concentration; <u>ceteris paribus</u>, the possibilities for concentration can be expected to decline with the differentiation of the product. $\underline{1}/$ Thus, it may be hypothesized that intra-industry trade will be negatively associated with industrial concentration. This hypothesis has been tested by utilizing the internationally adjusted concentration ratio introduced by Toh that is derived by dividing the traditional concentration ratio (the share of the largest four firms in the industry's output) by the share of imports in the industry's output. $\underline{2}/$

Finally, offshore assembly provisions may lead to increased intra-industry specialization by encouraging the international division of the production process, involving vertical specialization. Correspondingly, a positive correlation is hypothesized between offshore assembly and the extent of intra-industry trade. In the present investigation, the offshore assembly variable has been derived as the share of imports exempted from duties under offshore assembly provisions to total U.S. imports.

4.4 A Short Outline

Chapters 5 to 8 report on various investigations of intra-industry trade carried out in the framework of the present study. They consider first country characteristics affecting intra-industry trade, passing from the simpler to the more complicated, followed by industry characteristics, and

---

$\underline{1}/$ As Eastman and Stykolt note, a different conclusion would be reached if product differentiation raised entry barriers (1967, Ch. 1). For further discussion, see Caves, Porter, Spence, and Scott (1980, p. 44).

$\underline{2}/$ The explanation given by Toh for the negative sign he obtains is couched in terms of oligopolistic interdependence without reference

finally combining the two sets of characteristics.

Chapter 5 tests various hypotheses as to the country characteristics affecting intra-industry specialization in manufactured goods, by taking each country's trade with the rest of the world as the unit of observation. Chapter 6 investigates the country characteristics affecting this trade in a multilateral context. Chapter 7 introduces industry characteristics in testing various hypotheses as to the effects of these characteristics on the intra-industry trade of individual countries. Chapter 8 simultaneously introduces country and industry characteristics to test for their effects on intra-industry trade in a multi-country and multi-industry model.

Chapter 5

A CROSS COUNTRY ANALYSIS OF INTRA-INDUSTRY TRADE

5.1 The Hypotheses to be Tested

This chapter investigates the determinants of intra-industry trade in manufactured goods in a cross-country framework by taking the trade of individual countries with the rest of the world as the unit of observation. Its objective is to explain intercountry differences in the extent of intra-industry trade in manufactured goods by reference to the country characteristics affecting such trade. The investigation covers altogether 38 developed and developing countries that are major exporters of manufactured goods. Estimates are made for all the countries, taken together, as well as for 18 developed and for 20 developing countries. [1]

Reformulating the hypotheses described in Chapter 4, by reference to a country's trade with the rest of the world, it is hypothesized that the extent of intra-industry trade across countries will be

(1) positively correlated with per capita incomes, representing the extent of demand for differentiated products;

(2) positively correlated with country size, indicating the possibilities for increasing the variety of differentiated products manufactured under economies of scale;

(3) negatively correlated with average distance from the country's trading partners, representing the availability and the cost of information necessary for trading differentiated products;

(4) positively correlated with the existence of common borders with trading partners, indicating the possibilities for intra-industry

---

[1] For the list of countries, see Chapter 4.

trade in response to locational advantages;

(5) negatively correlated with the level of trade barriers, indicating the possibilities for intra-industry specialization under trade liberalization, and

(6) positively correlated with participation in regional integration schemes, such as the European Common Market, indicating the possibilities of intra-industry trade in the framework of regional integration scheme.

Section 5.2 presents the methodology applied. Section 5.3 reports the results obtained for the entire country group and makes comparisons with the results of other researchers. Estimates for developed and for developing countries are reported in Section 5.4. There is also a technical appendix.

5.2 The Methodology Applied

The index of intra-industry trade for a particular country (IIT_j) has been derived as in (5.1), where X_{ji}^e and M_{ji}^e, respectively, refer to the adjusted exports and imports of commodity i by country j. The formula makes adjustment for the imbalance in total trade, when X_j stands for total exports and M_j for total imports. [1] The index takes values from 0 and 1 as the extent of intra-industry trade increases. [2]

$$IIT_j = 1 - \frac{\sum_i |X_{ji}^e - M_{ji}^e|}{\sum_i (X_{ji}^e + M_{ji}^e)} = 1 - \frac{\sum_i \left| \frac{X_{ji}}{X_j} - \frac{M_{ji}}{M_j} \right|}{\sum_i \left(\frac{X_{ji}}{X_j} + \frac{M_{ji}}{M_j} \right)} \qquad (5.1)$$

where $X_{ji}^e = X_{ji} \frac{X_j + M_j}{2X_j}$ and $M_{ji}^e = M_{ji} \frac{X_j + M_j}{2M_j}$

---

[1] A consistent adjustment procedure was first proposed by Aquino (1978). However, while Aquino adjusted for the imbalance in trade in manufactured goods, in the present investigation adjustment has been made for the imbalance in total trade, so as to allow for inter-industry specialization between primary and manufactured goods (Balassa, 1979).

[2] We are indebted to Carl Christ for suggesting the transformation of equation (5.1) shown here.

The level of development has been defined as GNP per head (Y/P). [1] A dummy variable for developed and for developing countries has also been tried, but it has given poor statistical results. At any rate, the use of a continuous variable that recognizes the existence of gradation over the scale of economic development is preferable to a dummy variable that provides a binary classification.

Market size has been represented by the gross national product (Y). While the domestic consumption of manufactured goods would have been a more appropriate measure of the size of domestic market for these products, the necessary data are not available for several countries and are subject to considerable error for others. At the same time, from available information it appears that the consumption of manufactured goods and the gross national product are highly correlated.

Geographical distance has been introduced in the form of a variable for proximity. This has been defined as the weighted average of the inverse of distance (D) between country j and partner country k, the weights being the gross national product (Y) of the partner countries $\sum_k (Y_k/D_{jk}) / \sum_k Y_k$.

Trade orientation has been defined in terms of deviations of actual from hypothetical values of per capita exports as described in Chapter 4. The border trade variable has been given a value of 1 for countries that have a common border with at least one trading partner covered by the investigation. Dummy variables have also been introduced for membership in the European Common Market and the Latin American Free Trade Area, as well as for Singapore that has considerable entrepôt trade involving intra-industry specialization.

---

[1] GNP has been expressed in U.S. dollars by the use of market exchange rates. In a recent paper Noland (1987) showed that improved results can be obtained by using purchasing power parities as conversion ratio.

5.3 Empirical Results for the Entire Country Group

Three alternative estimation procedures have been used: ordinary least-squares, nonlinear least-squares utilizing a logistic function, and the logit analysis of the same logistic function with weighted least-squares. 1/

The three alternative estimation procedures have given similar results in terms of the statistical significance of the variables and the explanatory power of the regression equations, indicating the robustness of the estimates. 2/ The best statistical results are reported in Table 5.1.

The regression coefficients of income per head, the gross national product, the trade orientation variable, the proximity variable, and the Singapore dummy are all statistically significant at the 1 percent level in every equation while the border dummy is significant at least at the 5 percent level. However, the dummy variables for economic integration are not significant at even the 10 percent level in any of the equations, when combined with the above variables, and they have been dropped from the estimating equations.

The coefficient of determination is 0.90 using ordinary least-squares, 0.98 utilizing nonlinear least-squares, and 0.94 applying the logit procedure with weighted least-squares. In turn, the residual standard deviations, estimated as the sum of squares of the residuals divided by the number of observations, are 0.067, 0.066, and 0.067 in the three

---

1/ As noted in the Technical Appendix, the use of the latter estimation procedure has involved redefining the dependent variable of the regression equation. The logistic function is more appropriate in the present case as the dependent variable takes values between 0 and 1; use has also been made of ordinary least-squares, however, in part to test the sensitivity of the results to the choice of the estimation procedure and in part for comparability with other studies.

2/ This has also been the case in using the logit procedure with ordinary least-squares, the results of which are not reported here in order to economize with space.

Table 5.1

Estimates of Intra-Industry Trade

for Countries Exporting Manufactured Products

(regression coefficients with t-values in parenthesis)

	Ordinary Least Squares		Nonlinear Least Squares		Logit Analysis with Weighted Least Squares	
Constant	0.176	(5.26)	-1.604	(8.45)	-1.860	(9.41)
Proximity	0.141	(5.72)	0.611	(4.60)	0.617	(4.23)
Border Dummy	0.098	(2.90)	0.469	(2.07)	0.686	(4.34)
Per Capita GNP	0.061	(4.10)	0.377	(4.34)	0.464	(5.29)
GNP	0.054	(4.84)	0.204	(3.80)	0.271	(3.73)
Trade Orientation	0.128	(4.52)	0.612	(4.28)	0.703	(4.08)
Singapore Dummy	0.333	(3.95)	1.413	(3.94)	1.611	(2.74)
$\bar{R}^2$	0.8977		0.9784		0.9432	
$\hat{\sigma}$	0.0670		0.0659		0.0744	
N	38		38		38	

Note: For definition of variables and explanation of methodology, see text and Technical
Appendix. The proximity, per capita GNP and GNP variables, have been scaled in terms
of 10,000 miles, 1,000 dollars, and 100,000 dollars, respectively, and have been
expressed in natural logarithms.

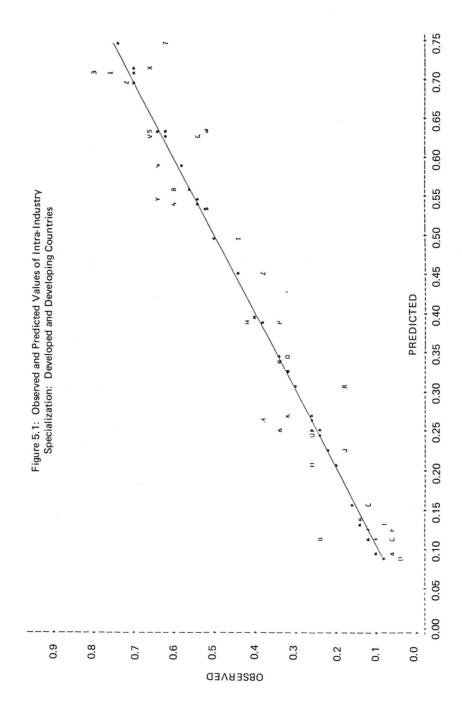

Figure 5.1: Observed and Predicted Values of Intra-Industry
Specialization: Developed and Developing Countries

cases, respectively. [1]

The plots obtained with the three alternative estimation procedures are also very similar and show uniformly small deviations from the regression line. Figure 5.1 shows the actual and predicted values of intra-industry trade under nonlinear least-squares estimation. As in the case of the other two methods of estimation, upward deviations are relatively more pronounced for India, Mexico, Austria and France while downward deviations are larger for Greece, Switzerland, and Germany. [2] The deviations may be attributed to random errors rather than to economic causes; given their smallness, a formal analysis of the residuals has not been attempted.

Table 5.2 compares the results obtained in a study by the Havrylyshyn and Civan (1983) by ordinary least-squares with estimates derived using the same specification in the present study, involving the introduction of an export concentration variable and EEC and NIC dummies. The regression equations explain three-fourths of the variance of the index of intra-industry trade in both cases and, with one exception, the statistical significance of the regression coefficients is also similar in the two studies.

The per capita income variable and the dummy variables for the European Common Market and for the newly-industrializing countries are statistically signficant at the 1 percent level whereas the market size variable is not significantly different from zero. However, while the variable for export concentration is significant at the 1 percent level in the Havrylyshyn-Civan study, it is not significantly different from zero

---

1/ For a discussion on the comparability of goodness of fit measures, see the Technical Appendix.

2/ See Table 1.1 for the symbols representing each country.

Table 5.2

Alternative Estimates of Intra-Industry Trade [a]

(regression coefficients; ordinary least-squares)

	Havrylyshyn Civan [c]		(1)		Present Study (2)		(3)		(4)	
Constant	0.1913	(3.44)	0.1702	(2.86)	0.0222	(0.38)	0.0120	(0.22)	0.0973	(1.78)
Proximity	-		-		0.0761	(2.37)	0.0935	(3.00)	0.1335	(4.62)
Border Dummy	-		-		0.1268	(3.02)	0.1154	(2.90)	0.0990	(2.83)
Per Capita GNP [b]	0.0038	(6.49)	0.0710	(7.04)	0.0619	(5.98)	0.0590	(6.01)	0.0390	(3.75)
GNP [b]	0.0015	(0.08)	-0.0084	(0.91)	-0.0003	(0.04)	0.0021	(0.28)	0.0432[d]	(3.02)
Trade Orientation	-		-		0.1045	(2.84)	0.1076	(3.11)	0.1236	(4.04)
Export Concentration	-0.2343	(2.74)	-0.6517	(1.44)	-0.3656	(0.99)	-0.2997	(0.86)	-0.2398	(0.79)
EEC Dummy	0.2683	(5.29)	0.2247	(3.78)	0.1259	(2.31)	0.1177	(2.29)	0.0442	(0.87)
NIC Dummy	0.1668	(4.95)	0.0936	(1.98)	0.0723	(1.86)	0.0569	(1.53)	0.0226	(0.66)
Singapore Dummy	-		-		-		0.2063	(2.20)	0.3293	(3.62)
$\bar{R}^2$	0.7663		0.7397		0.8305		0.8503		0.8868	
N	62		38		38		38		38	

Notes　(a) For definition of variables, see text.

(b) Gross domestic product in the Havrylyshyn-Civan study.

(c) For comparability with the present study the coefficient values have been divided by 100, with the exception of the per capita income variable where the same scaling was used in the two cases.

(d) Expressed in logarithmic terms.

in the present study. [1]

The high significance of the export concentration variable [2] in the Havrylyshyn–Civan study may be explained by the fact that these ~uthors included in the sample countries whose exports are dominated by a few primary export commodities. In fact, the export concentration variable and the per capita income variable, both representing the level of economic development in the country sample, dominate the results, with a coefficient of determination of 0.62 for the two variables alone.

This is hardly surprising since the Havrylyshyn–Civan study includes countries that have widely different economic structures, with a high extent of export concentration and a low share of manufactured exports being associated with a low level of intra–industry specialization. [3] Also, the choice made among low–income countries involves a considerable degree of arbitrariness, and the selection of a different set of countries might have given rise to different results. By contrast, the present study covers all manufacturing exporting countries that fulfil the criteria stated earlier.

In turn, the poor performance of the market size variable (GDP in the Havrylyshyn–Civan investigation and GNP in the present study) is explained by its introduction in an untransformed form. As shown in Table 5.2, this variable is highly significant statistically if expressed in logarithmic terms, which compresses the extreme observations and reduces the variability of GNP that is quite large compared to the variability of the

---

1/ Comparisons have not been made with the results obtained by Havrylyshyn–Civan in introducing dummy variables for the Latin American Free Trade Association and the Central American Free Trade Area, which were not significant at the 5 percent level in these authors' equations.

2/ This variable has been derived by calculating for each country the Herfindahl index.

3/ The 62 country sample used in the Havrylyshyn–Civan study includes countries such as Nigeria, the Central African Republic, Sudan, and Algeria, where manufactured exports do not reach 1 percent of their total exports.

index of intra-industry trade.

At the same time, the level of statistical significance of the EEC and the
NIC dummies declines if the proximity, border trade, and the Singapore
dummy variables are introduced in the estimating equations of the present
study. [1] And, these dummy variables are not significant statistically at
even the 10 percent level if the market size variable is expressed in
logarithmic terms.

It appears, then, that the use of EEC and NIC dummies involves a
misspecification as they pick up the statistical impact of other
variables. This conclusion is of particular interest as far as the Common
Market is concerned as it indicates that membership in the EEC adds little
to the effects of proximity and border trade on intra-industry
specialization, when the market size variable is expressed in logarithmis
terms. It further appears that the NIC dummy largely picks up the impact
of Singapore's entrepôt trade.

Finally, the model specification of the present study has successfully
included a policy variable in its effects on intra-industry specialization
that is absent from the Havrylyshyn-Civan study. The results obtained
with this variable indicate that increased openness, reflecting liberal
trade policies, leads to greater intra-industry trade. At the same time,
the specifications used in the present study have permitted explaining a
higher proportion of the variance of the extent of intra-industry trade
even though the countries under consideration represented a more
homogeneous group than in the Havrylyshyn-Civan investigation.

5.4 Empirical Results for Individual Groups of Countries

It has been noted that, in contradistinction with the Havrylyshyn-Civan
investigation, this study has been limited to countries exporting
manufactured products, thereby reducing the heterogeneity of the

---

[1] The exclusion of the trade orientation variable does not change this
result as this variable is uncorrelated with the other explanatory
variables.

observations. It has further been noted that the inclusion of a dummy variable for developed and for developing countries has given poor statistical results. At the same time, interest attaches to making separate estimates for developed and for developing country subgroups.

The separation of developed and developing economies has been effected by taking their 1973 per capita incomes as the benchmark. Countries with per capita incomes of $2254 or higher have been classified as developed and countries with per capita incomes of $2031 or lower as developing, with no country being between these two benchmarks.

The separation of the countries under study into two groups does not affect the explanatory power of the regression equation as represented by the coefficient of determination, under the nonlinear least squares procedure. For the developing country sample, this result obtains also under ordinary least squares estimation while the coefficient of determination is higher in this case if logit analysis with weighted least square is used. But the explanatory power of the regression is lower for the developed country sample under both the ordinary least squares and the logit procedures (Table 5.3). [1]

---

[1] The results are not directly comparable to those obtained by other writers who also analyzed the determinants of intra-industry trade among developed countries. Loertscher and Wolter (1980) used bilateral trade flows rather than each country's overall trade as observations. While this permitted testing for intercountry differences in per capita incomes and in market size, the coefficient of determination was only 0.15 and the results are marred by reason of the fact that, in using weighted least squares, the authors failed to weight the dependent variable. (For a correct application of a multilateral model, see Chapter 6 of this study.) Weighted least squares estimation was correctly used by Bergstrand (1983), but his investigation covered only SITC class 7 and the coefficient of determination of the regression equation is not reported. Clair, Gaussens, and Phan (1984) employed ordinary least squares in an equation pertaining to the intra-industry trade of the developed countries in SITC classes 5 and 7, with the coefficient of determination ranging between 0.66 and 0.74 in the reported estimates.

Table 5.3

Estimation of Intra-Industry Trade for Developed and for Developing Countries

Exporting Manufactured Products

	Ordinary Least Squares	Nonlinear Least Squares	Logit Analysis with Weighted Least Squares	Ordinary Least Squares	Nonlinear Least Squares	Logit Analysis with Weighted Least Squares
Constant	0.1276 (1.08)	-1.5872 (3.21)	-1.5443 (2.85)	0.2204 (3.99)	-1.3648 (3.21)	-1.7386 (4.42)
Proximity	0.1527 (2.41)	0.6236 (2.25)	0.7388 (2.64)	0.1414 (3.99)	0.6708 (3.02)	0.9974 (3.35)
Border Dummy	0.0268 (0.27)	0.1423 (0.33)	0.0441 (0.10)	0.0762 (2.25)	0.5787 (1.81)	0.6844 (3.19)
Per Capita GNP	0.1219 (1.55)	0.5254 (1.61)	0.4709 (1.30)	0.0198 (0.99)	0.1093 (0.74)	0.2828 (1.74)
GNP	0.0209 (0.80)	0.0813 (0.48)	0.1235 (1.04)	0.0917 (5.25)	0.5101 (4.22)	0.5469 (3.62)
Trade Orientation	0.2342 (1.25)	1.1302 (1.42)	0.7924 (0.93)	0.1485 (5.29)	0.9036 (4.10)	0.9791 (2.87)
Singapore Dummy	—	—	—	0.4570 (6.03)	2.2055 (4.96)	2.3371 (3.04)
$\bar{R}^2$	0.8122	0.9886	0.8445	0.9104	09.681	0.9784
s	0.0643	0.0624	0.0647	0.0446	0.0489	0.0657
N	18	18	18	20	20	20

Note: See Table 1.

In turn, the residual standard deviation is uniformly lower for the developing country sample and, to a much lesser extent, the developed country sample than for all countries taken together. At the same time, as explained in the Technical Appendix, it is the latter procedure rather than the coefficient of determination that permits comparisons of the goodness of fit under the different estimation procedures.

Notwithstanding the high explanatory power of the regression equations as countries exporting manufactured products have been divided into developed and developing country groups, increased intercorrelation among the explanatory variables and smaller variations in the values they take, have reduced the statistical significance of some of the regression coefficients. This is the case, in particular, in the developed country group where the gross national product and GNP per capita are highly correlated and there is little variation in several of the other variables.

Thus, the market size variable is not significant in any of the equations estimated for the developed country group, and the statistical significance of the per capita income variable barely approaches 10 percent. In turn, the proximity variable is statistically significant at the 5 percent level in all the equations, but the border variable is not significant at all. The latter result is explained by the fact that, apart from Australia and Japan, all developed countries have trading partners with common borders.

The trade orientation variable is not significant at the 10 percent level in the developed country equations. This result may be attributed to similarities among the developed countries as far as their trade orientation is concerned. With differences between actual and fitted values of per capita exports derived from equation (4.2) being relatively small, one cannot expect the trade orientation variable to be highly significant. [1]

By contrast, there are considerable variations among developing countries as far as their trade orientation is concerned, and the variable is statistically significant at the 1 percent level in all the equations. This is also the case for the proximity and the domestic market size variables and the Singapore dummy, while the per capita income variable is not significant at even the 10 percent level. Finally, the border dummy is statistically significant at the 5 percent level in the equation estimated by ordinary least-squares and at the 10 percent level in the other two equations.

Using the results of logit estimation, the hypothesis that the regression coefficients, taken jointly, are equal in the developed country, the developing country, and the combined, regressions is not rejected at the 5 percent level. The same conclusion holds for the coefficients, taken individually, the exception being the GNP variable.

Finally, as shown in Figures 5.2 and 5.3, the observed values of the index of intra-industry trade are close to their estimated values for both the developed and the developing country groups. This is the case, in particular, for the developing country group, with larger than average deviations shown for Portugal and Mexico in the upward, and for Spain in the downward, direction.

The differences are somewhat greater in the developed country group, where Australia and France show relatively large deviations in the upward, and Germany and Switzerland in the downward, direction. The deviations appear to largely correspond to those observed in making estimates for all the countries under consideration and do not appear to have a particular economic rationale; rather they can be attributed to random variations.

---

[1]   The standard deviation of the trade orientation variable, estimated from equation (4.2), is 0.19 for the developed country group and 0.62 for the developing country group.

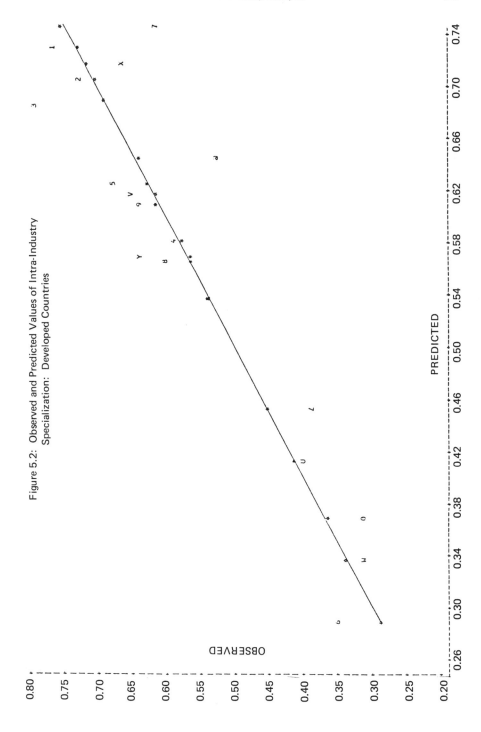

Figure 5.2: Observed and Predicted Values of Intra-Industry Specialization: Developed Countries

Part II

Figure 5.3: Observed and Predicted Values of Intra-Industry
Specialization: Developing Countries

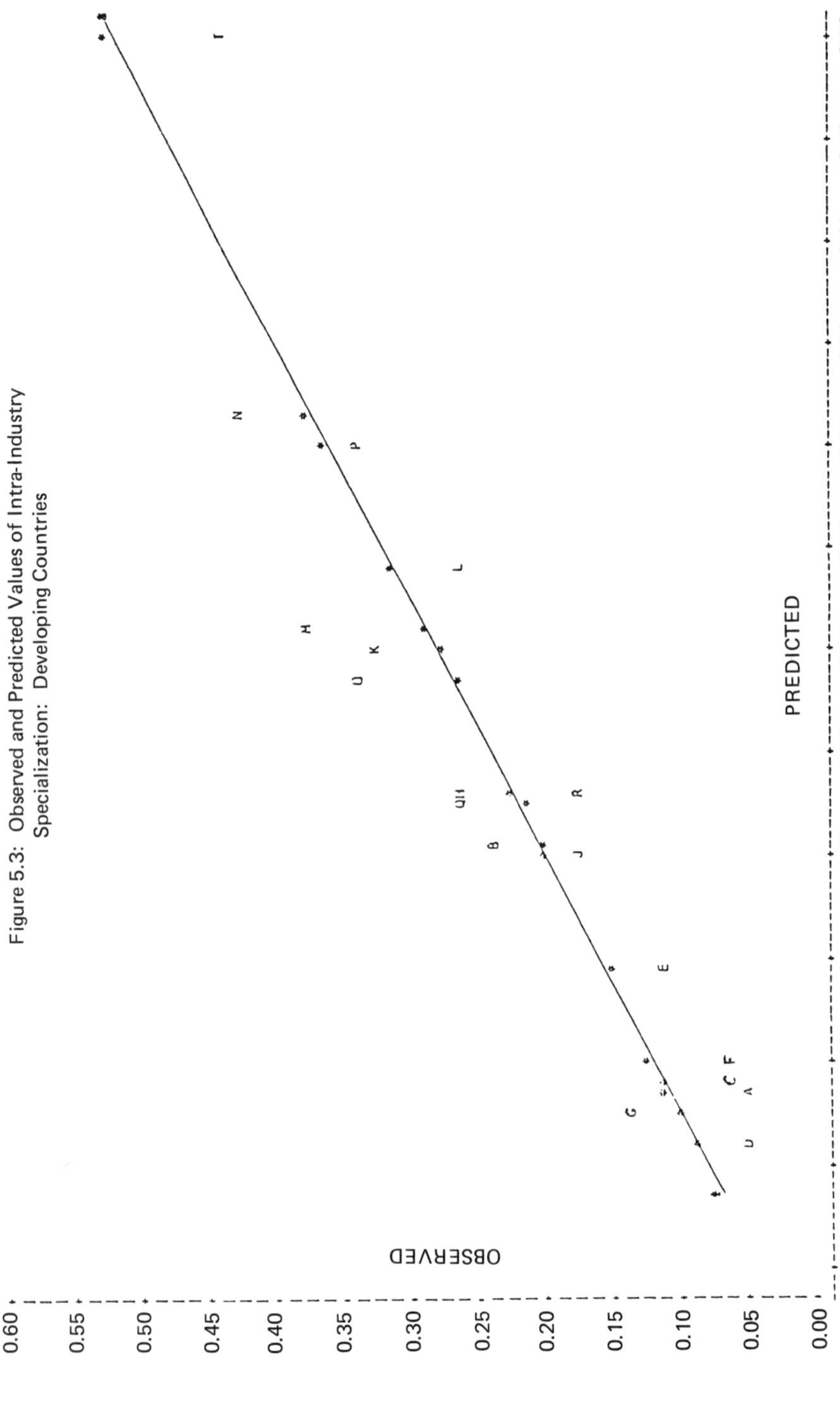

5.5 Summary

This chapter has set out to explain intercountry differences in the extent
of intra-industry trade in manufactured goods in the trade of individual
countries with the rest of the world by reference to hypotheses derived
from contributions to the theory of intra-industry trade. Apart from the
effects of economic integration on intra-industry specialization, all the
hypotheses put forward have been confirmed by the results and the
explanatory power of the regression equation is high, irrespective of the
estimating procedure used.

First of all, the extent of intra-industry specialization increases with
the level of economic development and the size of domestic markets. The
existence of trading partners with common borders and geographical
proximity also contribute to intra-industry trade and its role as an
entrepôt increases the extent of such trade in Singapore. Finally, intra-
industry specialization is positively associated with the openness of
national economies.

In turn, while according to the Havrylyshyn and Civan study participation
in integration arrangements and in the newly industrializing country group
contributes to the explanation of intra-industry specialization, this does
not appear to be the case if more appropriate specifications are
introduced. Thus, defining the market size variable in logarithmic terms,
the newly industrializing country dummy loses its statistical signficance
if the Singapore dummy is included in the regression equation and the same
fate befalls the Common Market dummy if allowance is made for border trade
and geographical proximity that appear to be the dominant variables.

Estimates have further been made by separating the countries under study
into developed and developing country groups. The explanatory power of
the regression equations and the statistical significance of the
coefficients in the developing country equations are again high. And
while similarities in regard to trade orientation and the existence of
border trade, as well as intercorrelation between the gross national
product and per capita GNP, reduce the statistical significance of the
regression coefficients of these variables for the developed country

group, the equations have a relatively high explanatory power.

At the same time, the developed country equation holds out the future for
the developing countries as far as intra-industry specialization is
concerned.   Approaching the problem differently, the overall equation
shows that rising per capita incomes in the process of economic
development lead to increased intra-industry trade.

Technical Appendix

Several alternative procedures have been tried to explain intercountry variations in the index of intra-industry trade (IIT) in the present study. This appendix discusses the choice of the functional form of the regression equation and methods of estimation utilized. It examines also the interpretation of the regression coefficients and the measures of goodness of fit under these procedures.

The index of intra-industry trade defined under (5.1) takes values between 0 and 1. There is no guarantee, however, that the predicted values of the regression equation will fall within this range whe linear (I) or log-linear functions are used while such an outcome is ensured if a logistic function is chosen as in (II). [1] The latter may also be transformed into (III), provided that the index of intra-industry trade is not exactly 0 or 1, which is the case for all the countries under consideration as indeed it is expected to be if the index pertains to individual countries. Under (III), the dependent variable (known as the logit of IIT) can vary between $-\infty$ and $+\infty$, and the regression equation is linear (in every case, x_j is defined as the vector of the explanatory variables).

(I) $IIT_j = \gamma' x_j$

(II) $IIT_j = 1/(1+\exp-\beta' x_j)$

(III) $\ln(IIT_j/1-IIT_j) = \beta' x_j$

Despite its possible disadvantages, (I) has been estimated by ordinary least-squares (OLS) as has been done by several researchers on intra-industry trade. [2] In turn, (II) has been estimated by the use of

---

[1] Other possible choices include the normal distribution function and the Gompertz curve, but they are not as convenient as the logistic function.

[2] In fact, the predicted values fall between 0 and 1 in the present study.

nonlinear least-squares (NLS) [1], while (III) has been estimated by ordinary least-squares as well as weighted least-squares (WLS). The latter method has been recommended for minimum chi-square estimation of the logit model in the case of multiple observations. [2] It has been applied by Loertscher and Wolter (1980) in the case of intra-industry trade, using $\sqrt{IIT_j \, (1-IIT_j)}$ to weight the explanatory variables. [3] This method has also been used in this study, although questions arise about the theoretical justification for this form of heteroscedasticity in the present context, and the results obtained show little evidence of its existence.

Next, we indicate how to interpret and compare estimates of the coefficients under the different specifications. Let $D_{jk}(x)$ denote the partial derivative of IIT_j with respect to x_{jk} (the k-th variable of x_j), while $E_{jk}(x)$ denotes the corresponding elasticity. Then, under (I),

$$D_{jk}(x) = \gamma_k \, , \, E_{jk}(x) = \gamma_k x_{jk}/IIT_j ,$$

while if $x_{jk} = \ln z_{jk}$,

$$D_{jk}(z) = \gamma_k/ z_{jk}, \, E_{jk}(z) = \gamma_k/ITT_j$$

Under (II) and (III),

1/ It should be noted that, in this case, NLS is equivalent to the maximum likelihood estimation (MLE) of (II) under the assumption that the disturbances are normal. However, such an assumption may be queried, since by construction the disturbances can only take values between -1 and +1. MLE could be performed by assuming that the disturbances have a truncated normal distribution, or a symmetrical beta distribution. Further research on this topic is in progress.

2/ In a model such as (III), IIT_j is an observed proportion, say n_j/m_j, where m_j is the number of observations corresponding to x_j, and n_j is the number of "successes". Then if m_j is large, the disturbance term of (III) has expectation 0 and variance $1/m_j$. IIT_j. $(1-IIT_j)$. The correction for heteroscedasticity thus requires dividing all the (dependent and explanatory) variables by the standard deviation of the disturbance and then applying OLS to the weighted data (Maddala, 1983, Chapter 2.8).

3/ However, they neglected to weight the dependent variables.

$$D_{jk}(x) = \beta_k \gamma_j \; , \; E_{jk}(x) = \beta_k \, x_{jk},$$

$$D_{jk}(z) = \beta_k \gamma_j / z_{jk}, \; E_{jk}(z) = \beta_k,$$

where $\gamma_j = \exp -\beta' x_j / (1 + \exp - \beta' x_j)^2$.

When a derivative or an elasticity depends on j, one can compute them at the sample mean of the relevant variables. [1] This has been done in the following example, with comparisons made for elasticities of the regression results reported in Table 1, when a subscript * indicates that the elasticity was computed at the sample mean.

	OLS	NLS	LOGIT(WLS)	LOGIT(OLS)
proximity	0.361*	0.611	0.550	0.557
per capita GNP	0.156*	0.377	0.347	0.414
GNP	0.138*	0.204	0.219	0.249
trade orientation	0.023*	0.043*	0.048*	0.047*

Finally, we consider how to compare the goodness of fit of the different estimation methods. The R^2 is the natural measure in the case of OLS applied to specification (I). In the case of NLS, we compute the ratio of the sums of squares of the predicted values and of the dependent variable, but this ratio is not strictly comparable to the R^2 of OLS, because the sum of squares in the denominator is the variance of IIT in the case of OLS. For the logit specification (III) by OLS or WLS, the R^2's are not comparable with those of OLS and NLS, since the dependent variable is not the same; they are not comparable between logit by OLS and WLS either because the dependent variable is weighted in the latter case but not in the former.

---

[1] An alternative method is to compute the sample mean of the derivatives or elasticities evaluated at the sample values.

An alternative procedure is to compare the four methods in terms of the standard deviation of the residuals of IIT. This standard deviation is obtained in a straightforward way in the cases of OLS with (I) and NLS with (II). In regard to (III), one has to use the estimates of β obtained by applying OLS or WLS to (III) in the right-hand side of (II) in order to compute the deviations between the two sides of (II). The resulting standard deviations will necessarily be greater than the standard deviation of OLS, since the latter method directly minimizes the sum of squares with respect to IIT, whereas the logit procedures minimize sums of squares with respect to the logit of IIT. The results are shown in Tables 5.1 to 5.3.

Chapter 6

INTRA-INDUSTRY TRADE AMONG EXPORTERS
OF MANUFACTURED GOODS

6.1 The Hypotheses to be Tested

This chapter examines the determinants of intra-industry specialization in
manufactured goods in bilateral trade, with reference to country
characteristics affecting this trade. While in Chapter 5 the trade of
individual countries with the rest of the world was the unit of
observation, in Chapter 6 it is trade between pairs of countries.

On the basis of the literature reviewed in Chapter 4, it is hypothesized
that the extent of intra-industry trade between any two countries will be

(1) positively correlated with their average per capita income,
     representing the extent of demand for differentiated products;

(2) negatively correlated with the differences between their per
     capita income, representing differences in their demand structure
     and/or difference in their resource endowments;

(3) positively correlated with their average size, indicating the
     possibilities for increasing the variety of differentiated
     products manufactured under economies of scale;

(4) negatively correlated with the difference between their size,
     indicating differences in their possibilities to manufacture
     differentiated products;

(5) negatively correlated with the distance between them,
     representing the availability and the cost of information
     necessary for trading differentiated product;

(6) positively correlated with the existence of common borders,

indicating the possibilities for intra-industry trade in response
to locational advantages.

(7) negatively correlated with their average level of trade barriers,
    indicating the possibilities for intra-industry specialization
    under trade liberalization;

(8) positively correlated with their joint participation in a
    regional integration scheme, including the European Common
    Market, the European Free Trade Association, and the Latin
    American Free Trade Association, indicating the possibilities of
    increased intra-industry trade in the framework of regional
    integration schemes, and

(9) positively correlated with the use of a common language,
    including English, French, Spanish, German, Portuguese, and
    Scandinavian (Danish, Norwegian, Swedish and Finnish).

Hypotheses (1) to (9) have been tested by defining the relevant variables
as in Chapter 4. Dummy variables have further been introduced to test for
the effects of U.K. and French colonial ties on the extent of an intra-
industry trade.

Section 6.2 describes the methodology applied. Sections 6.3 and 6.4
respectively, provide the results for the entire country group and for
individual groups of countries, including trade among developed countries,
among developing countries, and between developed and developing
countries. Section 6.4 also tests for the statistical significance of
differences in the results obtained for various groups of countries.
Finally, the technical appendix makes comparisons with the results
obtained by other authors.

6.2 The Methodology Applied

The index of intra-industry trade for any pair of countries (IIT_{jk}) has
been derived as in (6.1) where X^e_{jki} and M^e_{jki} refer to the adjusted
exports and imports of commodity i in trade between countries j and k. The
formula makes adjustment for imbalance in total trade between any pair of
countries, when X_{jk} and M_{jk} respectively, stand for the total exports

and imports of country j in trade with country k. [1] The index takes values from 0 to 1 as the extent of intra-industry trade increases.

$$IIT_{jk} = 1 - \frac{\sum_i | X^e_{jki} - M^e_{jki} |}{\sum_i (X^e_{jki} + M^e_{jki})} = 1 - \frac{\sum_i \left| \dfrac{X_{jki}}{X_{jk}} - \dfrac{M_{jki}}{M_{jk}} \right|}{\sum_i \left(\dfrac{X_{jki}}{X_{jk}} + \dfrac{M_{jki}}{M_{jk}} \right)} \qquad (6.1)$$

where $X^e_{jki} = X_{jki} \dfrac{X_{jk} + M_{jk}}{2X_{jk}}$ and $M^e_{jki} = M_{jki} \dfrac{X_{jk} + M_{jk}}{2M_{jk}}$

A linear or loglinear regression equation may give estimated values that lie outside the 0 to 1 range. A logistic function, defined in (6.2), does not have this shortcoming; [2] however, its logit transformation [3] cannot handle values of 0 or 1. Since a value of zero provides relevant information, representing the extreme case of inter-industry specialization, (6.2) has been estimated by nonlinear least squares in the

---

1/ A consistent adjustment procedure was first proposed by Aquino (1978). However, while Aquino adjusted for the imbalance of trade in manufactured goods, in the present investigation adjustment has been made for the imbalance in total trade, so as to allow for inter-industry specialization between primary and manufactured goods. This procedure was introduced in Balassa, 1979; in the present investigation, the adjustment has been made on a bilateral basis as has also been done by Bergstand (1983). On the choice of the method of adjustment, see also Greenaway and Milner (1981).

2/ This shortcoming is of particular relevance to the use of the model for predictive purposes and for comparisons of actual and estimated values. But, in any case, it is desirable to choose a functional form for the estimating equation that conforms to the structure of the data; otherwise, the estimates and their covariance matrix may be distorted and lead to incorrect conclusions in accepting or rejecting hypotheses.

3/ The logit transformation is $\ln(IIT_{jk}/1 - IIT_{jk}) = \beta' z_{jk}$.

present investigation. $\underline{1/}$

$$IIT_{jk} = \frac{1}{1 + \exp - \beta' z_{jk}},$$ (6.2)

where z_{jk} is the vector of the explanatory variables.

6.3   Empirical Results for the Entire Country Group

The empirical estimates for the entire group of 38 countries are reported
in Table 6.1.   Equation (6.3) shows the results of estimation including
the common characteristics of the countries cited in Section 6.1 (cf. also
Table 4.1), together with dummy variables for economic integration, common
language, and colonial ties.   In equation (6.4) those variables of
equation (6.3) have been retained that were statistically significant at
least at the 10 percent level.   Finally, equation (6.5) includes common
country characteristics only.

The results support the hypotheses put forward in Section 6.1 regarding
all the common characteristics of the countries in question.   Thus, the
regression coefficients of the average per capita income (AY/P), income
inequality (INEQ Y/P), average country size (AY), inequality in country
size (INEQY), trade orientation (ATO), distance (D), and border (BORDER)
variables all have the expected sign and are statistically significant at
the 1 percent level in equations (6.3) to (6.5).

Among the economic integration variables, the EFTA and the LAFTA dummies
have the expected sign and are statistically significant at the 1 percent
level.   In turn, the EEC dummy has the expected sign, but is not
significant even at the 10 percent level.   While this may seem surprising
in view of the emphasis given to intra-industry specialization in the
European Common Market from the mid-sixties (Balassa, 1966) onwards, the
results appear to indicate that general country characteristics, including

---

$\underline{1/}$ There are 99 cases where IIT_{jk} is 0 because either X_{jki} or M_{jki} is
equal to zero for all commodities; in no case is IIT_{jk} equal to 1.

Table 6.1

Estimates of Intra Industry Trade for Countries Exporting

Manufactured Products: Developed and Developing Countries Combined

(regression coefficients, with t-values in parenthesis)

	Equation (6.3)		Equation (6.4)		Equation (6.5)	
Constant	3.140	(11.21)	3.216	(11.78)	3.151	(11.36)
$\ln AY/P$	0.662	(8.62)	0.670	(8.82)	0.698	(9.52)
INEQ Y/P	-1.115	(6.62)	-1.106	(6.60)	-1.214	(6.92)
$\ln AY$	0.400	(11.84)	0.407	(12.40)	0.368	(11.46)
INEQY	-0.820	(7.31)	-0.847	(7.76)	-0.818	(7.23)
ATO	0.483	(10.54)	0.492	(10.93)	0.494	(10.98)
$\ln D$	-0.525	(19.43)	-0.532	(20.24)	-0.531	(20.04)
BORDER	0.331	(3.69)	0.381	(4.89)	0.400	(4.94)
EEC	0.154	(1.28)	-	-	-	-
EFTA	0.368	(4.37)	0.371	(4.89)	-	-
LAFTA	2.047	(6.74)	2.050	(6.79)	-	-
ENGLISH	0.233	(2.26)	0.218	(2.12)	-	-
SPANISH	1.400	(5.14)	1.413	(5.21)	-	-
FRENCH	0.081	(0.25)	-	-	-	-
GERMAN	0.107	(0.56)	-	-	-	-
PORT.	0.024	(0.02)	-	-	-	-
SCAND.	0.068	(0.46)	-	-	-	-
FRCOL	-0.141	(0.21)	-	-	-	-
UKCOL	0.457	(2.00)	0.473	(2.07)	-	-
$\bar{R}^2$	0.8721		0.8772		0.8573	
$\hat{\sigma}$	0.0707		0.0705		0.0741	
N	684		684		684	

Note: For the definition of the variables and explanation of methodology, see Table 4.1.

the border variable, largely explain the extent of intra-industry trade
among the Common Market countries. $\underline{1}$/

The English and Spanish language variables have the expected sign and are
statistically significant at the 1 percent level whereas the other
language dummies have very low t-values. The latter conclusion also
applies to the French colonial ties variable which has a negative sign; in
turn, the variable for English colonial ties has the expected positive
sign and it is statistically significant at the 5 percent level.

The French language and colonial ties variables are highly intercorrelated
as the former includes the latter plus Belgium and Switzerland. $\underline{2}$/ At the
same time, the results are not affected if only one or the other of the
variables is included in the estimating equation. It would, then, appear
that trade ties between France and its former colonies largely involves
inter-industry specialization.

6.4 Empirical Results for Individual Groups of Countries

Table 6.2 provides the results obtained for intra-industry trade among
developed countries. Equation (6.6) includes all the relevant variables;
it omits the dummies for LAFTA, Spanish and Portuguese languages, and
colonial ties, which are not relevant for trade among these countries.
Equation (6.7) also excludes variables whose level of statistical
significance did not reach 10 percent while equation (6.8) incorporates
only the common country characteristics.

With the exception of intercountry differences in per capita income
levels, the results support the hypotheses confirmed by the estimates for
the entire group of countries. However, apart from the EEC dummy, the
statistical significance of the coefficients is lower than in the previous
case, and two variables (ln AY/P and BORDER) are significant at only the 5

1/ These results reconfirm those of Chapter 5.

2/ The existence of intercorrelation may provide an explanation for the
negative sign of the French colonial ties variable.

Table 6.2

Estimates of Intra Industry Trade for Countries Exporting
Manufactured Products: Trade among Developed Countries
(regression coefficients, with t-values in parenthesis)

	Equation (6.6)		Equation (6.7)		Equation (6.8)	
Constant	2.299	(2.82)	2.243	(2.87)	2.497	(3.10)
$\ln$ AY/p	0.596	(2.32)	0.660	(2.69)	0.680	(2.66)
INEQ Y/P	-0.775	(0.77)	-	-	-0.548	(0.53)
$\ln$ AY	0.298	(3.99)	0.299	(4.07)	0.277	(3.82)
INEQY	-0.579	(2.84)	-0.608	(3.05)	-0.677	(3.34)
ATO	0.792	(3.20)	0.765	(3.26)	0.738	(2.98)
$\ln$ D	-0.445	(8.95)	-0.452	(9.28)	-0.478	(9.64)
BORDER	0.265	(2.11)	0.343	(3.14)	0.401	(3.59)
EEC	0.252	(1.65)	0.210	(1.46)	-	-
EFTA	0.353	(3.13)	0.404	(3.99)	-	-
ENGLISH	0.271	(1.74)	0.244	(1.59)	-	-
FRENCH	0.037	(0.09)	-	-	-	-
GERMAN	0.226	(0.95)	-	-	-	-
SCAND.	0.218	(1.13)	-	-	-	-
$\bar{R}^2$	0.9467		0.9458		0.9390	
$\hat{\sigma}$	0.0846		0.0841		0.0886	
N	153		153		153	

Note See Table 6.1

percent and one variable (English) at the 10 percent level.

The lack of statistical significance of the variable representing intercountry differences in per capita incomes may be explained by the fact that, with income differences being much smaller among developed countries than in the entire group of countries, the demand structure of the countries concerned is also more similar. Correspondingly, one may not expect large variations to occur in the extent of intra-industry trade as a function of income differences.

In turn, the lower level of significance of the English language variable may be attributed to the fact that several of the English-speaking countries are in the developing country sample. Finally, the EEC dummy is (barely) significant at the 10 percent level in equation (6.6), indicating the increased relevance of this variable once developing countries are omitted from the calculations.

The level of significance of the EEC dummy variable (slightly) falls below the benchmark in equation (6.7) that excludes the variables which were not significant at the 10 percent level as in equation (6.6). The same fate befalls the English language variable, but again by a small margin.

By contrast, the EFTA dummy remains statistically significant at the 1 percent level. Also, the level of significance of the average per capita income and the border variables improves to 1 percent as the variables that were not significant at the 10 percent level are eliminated from the estimating equation. These results are not affected if only the variables representing the common country characteristics are retained as in equation (6.8).

The EEC, EFTA, the German and Scandanavian language, and the colonial ties variables have been omitted from equation (6.9), estimated for intra-industry trade among developing countries and reported in Table 6.3. The per capita income inequality variable is again not statistically significant, reflecting considerations similar to those adduced for the developed country group. Apart from this variable, the results again support the hypotheses confirmed for the entire group of 38 countries,

Table 6.3

Estimates of Intra Industry Trade for Countries Exporting

Manufactured Products: Trade among Developing Countries

(regression coefficients, with t-values in parenthesis)

	Equation (6.9)		Equation (6.10)		Equation (6.11)	
Constant	5.121	(3.92)	4.782	(3.76)	6.738	(5.80)
$\ln$ AY/P	1.117	(4.02)	1.291	(5.11)	1.349	(4.53)
INEQ Y/P	-0.564	(0.98)	-	-	-0.283	(0.50)
$\ln$ AY	0.872	(3.57)	0.807	(3.43)	1.356	(7.56)
INEQY	-1.592	(2.14)	-1.522	(2.11)	-3.344	(5.73)
ATO	0.875	(7.88)	0.869	(8.26)	1.031	(8.65)
$\ln$ D	-0.609	(5.79)	-0.611	(6.03)	-0.531	(5.04)
BORDER	0.880	(2.48)	0.821	(2.38)	1.118	(3.84)
LAFTA	2.187	(5.56)	2.274	(5.80)	-	-
ENGLISH	0.776	(3.33)	0.641	(3.18)	-	-
SPANISH	1.556	(3.90)	1.610	(4.02)	-	-
FRENCH	0.404	(0.05)	-	-	-	-
PORT.	0.620	(0.55)	-	-	-	-
$\bar{R}^2$	0.7402		0.7385		0.6671	
$\hat{\sigma}$	0.0501		0.0498		0.0558	
N	175		175		175	

Note: See Table 6.1.

although the inequality in country size and the border variables are significant at only the 5 percent level.

The LAFTA and the Spanish and English language dummies are statistically significant at the 1 percent level, representing an improvement in the case of the latter variable over the previous results. In turn, if these variables are omitted as in equation (6.11), the level of significance of the inequality in country size and the border variables improves to 1 percent.

Finally, all the variables representing the common characteristics of the countries concerned are statistically significant at the 1 percent level in equation (6.12) that provides estimates for intra-industry trade between developed and developing countries (Table 6.4). Among the dummy variables for economic integration, common language, and colonial ties, the EFTA dummy pertaining to trade between the developed member countries and Portugal is significant at the 10 percent level while the French language and the British colonial ties variables reach this level of significance under some specifications but not under others. [1]

It is apparent that, apart from the income inequality variable that loses its statistical significance in cases where the intercountry variation of incomes is more limited, the variables representing the common characteristics of the countries concerned are highly significant statistically, regardless of the choice of the country sample or the specifications of the estimating equations. Several of the variables pertaining to economic integration, common language, and colonial ties are also statistically significant but, with the exception of the developing country group, they add little to the explanatory power of the equations. Also, the coefficient of determination remains practically unaffected if variables whose level of significance does not reach 10 percent are omitted from the regression equations.

---

[1] With the French language and French colonial ties variables being highly correlated, the former loses its statistical significance if the latter is omitted from the estimating equation. Correspondingly, both have been dropped from equation (6.13).

Table 6.4

Estimates of Intra Industry Trade for Countries Exporting

Manufactured Products: Trade between Developed and Developing Countries

(regression coefficients, with t-values in parenthesis)

	Equation (6.12)		Equation (6.13)		Equation (6.14)	
Constant	2.749	(5.59)	2.693	(5.61)	2.591	(5.45)
ℓn AY/P	0.741	(3.63)	0.765	(3.81)	0.768	(3.86)
INEQ Y/P	-1.373	(5.48)	-1.322	(5.33)	-1.383	(5.58)
ℓn AY	0.408	(6.34)	0.403	(6.28)	0.378	(6.03)
INEQY	-0.635	(2.79)	-0.622	(2.77)	-0.561	(2.50)
ATO	0.333	(4.38)	0.348	(4.70)	0.358	(4.91)
ℓn D	-0.483	(9.38)	-0.482	(9.54)	-0.476	(9.65)
BORDER	0.789	(4.08)	0.785	(4.06)	0.787	(4.06)
EFTA	0.354	(1.71)	0.343	(1.66)	-	-
ENGLISH	0.165	(0.81)	-	-	-	-
FRENCH	0.982	(2.17)	-	-	-	-
FRCOL	-0.010	(1.37)	-	-	-	-
UKCOL	0.541	(1.50·)	0.675	(2.08)	-	-
$\bar{R}^2$	0.6993		0.6966		0.6920	
$\hat{\sigma}$	0.0713		0.0713		0.0717	
N	356		356		356	

Note: See Table 6.1

The coefficient of determination [1] is the highest (0.95) in the equation explaining intra-industry trade among developed countries. This result is of particular interest in view of the fact that, as first suggested by Linder, the extent of intra-industry specialization is much greater in trade among developed countries than in trade among developing countries or between developed and developing countries. [2] At the same time, it is noteworthy that the explanatory power of the regression equation is high, with coefficients of determination of 0.74 and 0.70, in the latter two cases also; it is 0.87 in the equation pertaining to the entire group of countries. [3]

6.5 Summary

Various hypotheses put forward in the theoretical literature as regards the determinants of intra-industry specialization have been tested in this paper for trade among countries exporting manufactured goods. This has been done in regard to trade among all the countries meeting certain criteria, as well as for trade among developed countries, among developing countries, and between developed and developing countries.

The results show that the extent of intra-industry trade between any two countries increases with their average income level, represented by per capita GNP, and with their average size, represented by GNP, and it decreases with differences in their income level and in their size. However, differences in income levels are not significantly related to the extent of intra-industry specialization in trade among developed and among developing countries, where income differences are much smaller than

---

[1] On the definition of the coefficient of determination in case of estimation by nonlinear least squares, see the Technical Appendix to Chapter 5.

[2] The average index of intra-industry trade is 0.300 for trade among developed countries, 0.039 for trade among developing countries, 0.081 for trade between developed and developing countries, and 0.120 for trade among all countries covered.

[3] The differences in the results cannot be explained by the adjustment procedure applied to define the index of intra-industry trade as the use of unadjusted data shows a similar pattern.

between developed and developing countries.

It further appears that the extent of intra-industry trade is positively correlated with the trade orientation of the countries concerned as well as with the existence of a common border and it is negatively correlated with the distance between them. Taken together, these common country characteristics explain much of the variation in the extent of intra-industry specialization, with the coefficient of determination ranging from 0.95 for trade among developed countries to 0.67 for trade among developing countries.

Introducing variables for economic integration, common language, and colonial ties increases the explanatory power of the regression equations relatively little, the exception being the equation for trade among developing countries. At the same time, several of these variables are highly significant statistically. Thus, it is apparent that participation in the European Free Trade Association and in the Latin American Free Trade Association increases the extent of intra-industry trade. The regression coefficient for EEC membership is also positive, but its level of statistical significance rarely reaches 10 percent. Finally, English and Spanish as common languages and English colonial ties appear to contribute to intra-industry specialization.

While the statistical significance of the estimates for the various country groups is generally high, the regression coefficients of several of the variables vary among the groups. The statistical significance of these differences has been tested in regard to the three subgroups by utilizing the results obtained in equations (6.8), (6.11), and (6.14) that contain common country characteristics, so as to ensure comparability in the results.

As shown in equations (6.15), (6.16), and (6.17), the differences in the regression coefficients are not statistically significant in regard to the average per capita GNP, income inequality, and distance variables at the 10 percent level, and in regard to the border variables at the 5 percent level, in any of the three comparisons (Table 6.5). Nor are there statistically significant differences at the 5 percent level in regard to

Table 6.5

Differences between Regression Coefficients
Estimated in the Three Subgroups [a]

(with t-values in parenthesis)

	Trade among developing countries and trade among developed countries		Trade between developed and developing countries and trade among developed countries		Trade between developed and developing countries and trade among developing countries	
	Equation (6.15)		Equation (6.16)		Equation (6.17)	
Constant	4.241	(2.58)	0.094	(0.12)	−4.148	(2.62)
$\ln AY/P$	0.669	(1.53)	0.088	(0.31)	−0.581	(1.34)
INEQ Y/P	0.264	(0.24)	−0.836	(0.95)	−1.100	(1.42)
$\ln AY$	1.079	(4.50)	0.101	(1.17)	−0.978	(4.07)
INEQY	−2.667	(3.45)	0.116	(0.42)	2.783	(3.53)
ATO	0.293	(1.15)	−0.380	(1.77)	−0.673	(3.94)
D	−0.052	(0.37)	0.002	(0.03)	0.055	(0.38)
BORDER	0.717	(1.85)	0.386	(1.79)	−0.331	(0.78)
joint test [b]		31.38		11.07		35.05

Notes: (a) The differences are derived from pairwise comparisons between equations (6.8), (6.11), and (6.14).

(b) The statistic for the joint test of equality is distributed as a chi-square random variable, with eight degrees of freedom.

any of the variables if the estimates for intra-industry trade between developed and developing countries and among developed countries are compared. However, differences in the regression coefficients of the average country size and the size inequality variables are significant at the 1 percent level in the other two comparisons. The same conclusion applies to the trade orientation variable, when the estimates for trade between developed and developing countries and among developing countries are compared.

In addition to testing the statistical significance of differences between the individual regression coefficients, combined tests for these coefficients have also been carried out. As is apparent from the results of Table 6.5, the hypothesis that the regression coefficients, taken jointly, are equal is rejected in the comparisons of the equation pertaining to intra-industry trade among developing countries with the other two equations; it is accepted in the comparison of the estimates for trade among developed countries and between developed and developing countries.

Almost twenty years ago one of the authors analyzed the benefits of intra-industry trade through the increased exchange of consumer goods and specialization in narrower ranges of machinery and intermediate products. These benefits include greater satisfaction of consumer needs as well as the exploitation of economies of scale through the lengthening of production runs (Balassa, 1966).

It is apparent that developing countries can increasingly obtain the benefits of intra-industry trade as they reach higher levels of economic development. At the same time, the findings of the investigation point to the conclusion that these benefits can be augmented through the liberalization of trade that contributes to intra-industry trade.

Technical Appendix

Comparisons with Estimates by Loertscher and Wolter

The only comparable estimates of the determinants of intra-industry
specialization in bilateral trade are those by Loertscher and Wolter
(1980) who made calculations for OECD countries other than Australia and
New Zealand. 1/ Table 6 reports the Loertscher-Wolter results, together
with estimates for the same group of countries derived by using the data
of this study.

In order to ensure comparability, the variables used in the present study
have been redefined to correspond to those of Loertscher and Wolter. This
has involved using absolute differences of per capita GNP (DY/P) and GNP
(DY) in the place of the inequality measures, omitting the trade
orientation variable, and combining the dummy variables for economic
integration (EI) and common languages (CL). However, a cultural group
(CG) dummy variable has not been included because of its intercorrelation
with the language variable.

In interpreting the estimates, it should be noted that the index of intra-
industry trade used by Loertscher and Wolter (P_{jk}) is scaled to vary
between 0 and 100. Furthermore, in applying logit analysis with weighted
least squares, Loertscher and Wolter weighted the independent but not the
dependent variables by $[P_{jk}(100 - P_{jk})]^{\frac{1}{2}}$. This is incorrect and in the
estimates reported in equation (6.19) the dependent variable has also been
appropriately weighted. At the same time, as noted below, the coefficient
values and their level of significance are affected to a considerable
extent if the incorrect weighting procedure is used.

Table 6.6 further reports the results obtained by nonlinear least squares

---

1/ The authors used data for 59 out of 102 three-digit SITC categories to
    compute the index of intra-industry trade, utilizing equation 6.1
    reported in the text, except that they made adjustment for imbalance
    in bilateral trade in manufactured goods rather than total trade as
    noted above.

Table 6.6

Estimates of Intra-Industry Trade among Developed Countries

(regression coefficients, with t-values in parenthesis)

	Loertscher-Wolter [a] weighted least squares		This study			
			weighted least squares		nonlinear least squares	
	Equation (6.18)		Equation (6.19)		Equation (6.20)	
Constant	-78.300	(n.a.)	1.855	(3.75)	2.419	(5.03)
$\ln AY/P$	-0.210	(0.25)	0.877	(6.06)	0.954	(6.60)
$\ln DY/P$	-0.436	(8.92)	-0.075	(1.89)	-0.063	(1.66)
$\ln AY$	0.619	(7.85)	0.580	(6.47)	0.617	(7.25)
$\ln DY$	-0.251	(2.67)	-0.246	(4.34)	-0.243	(4.73)
$\ln D$	-0.408	(5.59)	-0.438	(9.28)	-0.527	(11.05)
Border	0.094	(0.03)	0.259	(1.93)	0.195	(1.61)
EI	0.535	(2.12)	0.385	(2.36)	0.418	(2.77)
CL	0.166	(0.09)	0.286	(2.13)	0.342	(2.80)
CG	0.363	(0.99)	n.a.		n.a.	
$\bar{R}^2$	0.147		0.798		0.927	
$\hat{\sigma}$	n.a.		0.089 [b]		0.088	
N	187		190		190	

Note: (a) All the regression coefficients should be multiplied by 10^{-2}. This is explained by the scaling of the index of intra-industry trade and the lack of weighting of the dependent variable.

    (b) Standard deviation of the differences between the observed values of IIT_{jk} and the estimated values computed by using the estimates of equation (6.19).

estimation of the logistic function as used elsewhere in this investigation (cf. Section 6.3). The results show that the average size variable, the size differential variable, as well as the distance variable are statistically significant at the 1 percent level in all the equations. The per capita income differential variable is also significant at the 5 percent level in the present study. In turn, the average per capita income variable is not significant in the Loertscher-Wolter study while it is significant at the 1 percent level in the estimates of this study. Among the remaining variables, the economic integration dummy is statistically significant at the 5 percent level in the estimates derived by weighted least squares in both studies whereas the common language dummy is significant at the 1 percent level in the nonlinear least squares, and at the 5 percent level in the weighted least squares, estimates of this study and not at all in the Loertscher-Wolter study. [1]

---

[1] Applying the incorrect weighting procedure used by Loertscher and Woltker to the data of the present study, the average per capita income, average size and distance variables are significant at the 1 percent level, the differential size variable barely attains the 10 percent level of significance while the other variables are far from reaching this level. Furthermore, the absolute values of the coefficients are affected to a considerable extent, although all retain the expected sign. Finally, the standard error of the implied residuals is 0.146, while the adjusted coefficient of determination drops to 0.462. The latter value is nonetheless much higher than in the Loertscher-Wolter results (0.147).

Chapter 7

INDUSTRY CHARACTERISTICS AND INTRA-INDUSTRY TRADE

7.1 The Hypotheses to be Tested

Chapters 5 and 6 analyzed the determination of intra-industry trade in manufactured goods by reference to the country characteristics affecting such trade. In Chapter 5 this was done by taking the country as the unit of observation; in Chapter 6 bilateral trade was considered.

The present chapter will introduce industry characteristics in examining the determinants of the intra-industry trade in manufactured goods for individual countries. The calculations pertain to the industry and country characteristics affecting intra-industry trade in the United States, France, Germany, the United Kingdom, and Japan.

The industry characteristics utilized in the investigation pertain to the United States and orginate in the work of Caves (1981), with the addition of variables for industrial concentration and offshore assembly. The country characteristics were described in the previous chapter.

On the basis of the literature reviewed in Chapter 4, it is hypothesized that the extent of intra-industry trade in the products of a particular industry will be

(1) positively correlated with the degree of product differentiation;
(2) negatively correlated with the degree of product standardization;
(3) positively correlated with offshore assembly.

Hypothesis (1) has been tested by defining product differentiation in terms of (a) the coefficient of variation of export unit values (Hufbauer, 1970); and (b) marketing expenditures expressed as a percentage of total costs (Caves, 1981);

Hypothesis (2) has been tested by defining product standardization in terms of (a) the extent of plant economies of scale, [1] measured by dividing the ratio of the average size of shipments of the largest plant in U.S. industry, accounting for approximately one-half of industry shipment, to total industry shipment, by the ratio of value added per worker in smaller plants, again accounting for one-half of industry shipments, to value added per worker in larger plants (Caves, 1981) [2] and (b) the extent of industry concentration, measured by the share of the largest four firms in an industry's output, divided by the share of imports in industry output (Toh, 1982). [3]

Hypothesis (3) has been tested by utilizing data on the relative importance of offshore assembly in individual industries in the United States.

In the investigation, industry characteristics have been introduced together with country characteristics relating the country under consideration to other countries. The hypotheses pertaining to country characteristics are again based on the literature reviewed in Chapter 4.

---

[1] While plant economies of scale have been interpreted to reflect the extent of product standardization, an appropriate measure could not be devised for the length of the production run that represents economies of scale in differentiated products, which are considered to contribute to intra-industry trade in the theoretical literature (cf. Chapter 4).

[2] Caves expects a negative sign for this variable on the grounds that extensive economies of scale would confine production to a few locations.

[3] While Toh considers this measure to reflect the oligopolistic interdependence of industries, it can be assumed to be positively correlated with the degree of product standardization.

It is hypothesized that the extent of intra-industry trade for any pair of countries will be

    (4)   negatively correlated with the differences between their per capita income, representing differences in their demand structure and/or their resource endowments;

    (5)   negatively correlated with the difference between their size, indicating differences in their possibilities to manufacture differentiated products;

    (6)   negatively correlated with their average level of trade barriers, indicating the possibilities for intra-industry specialization under trade liberalization; and

    (7)   negatively correlated with the distance between them, representing the availability and cost of information necessary for trading differentiated products.

Per capita income is measured by GNP per head and country size by GNP; they are introduced in the form of the inequality measure described in Chapter 4. Chapter 4 also describes the trade orientation variable that is used to indicate the extent of trade barriers. Finally, geographical distance is measured between centers of geographical gravity in each country.

Section 7.2 describes the methodology applied. The empirical results are presented in Section 7.3 for the United States, for which several alternative methods of estimation are used. In Section 7.4, the method of estimation, which is considered to be most appropriate for the present investigation, is further applied to France, Germany, the United Kingdom, and Japan.

7.2 The Methodology Applied

The investigation pertains to manufactured goods, with the exclusion of natural resource products whose manufacture is importantly affected by the availability of natural resources in a particular country. As explained in Chapter 4, the commodity classification scheme utilized has been established on the basis of the United States Standard Industrial

Classification, with 4-digit SIC categories merged in cases when the
economic characteristics of particular products have been judged to be
very similar. The application of this procedure has led to the choice of
altogether 167 industry categories that have been matched with the 3- and
4-digit categories of the UN Standard International Trade Classification
(SITC). However, 15 categories had to be dropped for lack of data on
industry characteristics at the required level of disaggregation.

The investigation covers 37 trading partners of the United States, each of
which had manufactured exports of at least \$300 million, accounting for 18
percent or more of total exports, in 1979. Data on U.S. trade in a
particular industry with a particular country have been taken as the unit
of observation.

The formula utilized in deriving the index of intra-industry trade (IIT)
is shown in equation (7.1) that makes adjustment for imbalance in the
total trade of the United States with individual countries. [1/] X_{ji} and
M_{ji} refer to U.S. exports and imports of commodity i in trade with
country j while X_j and M_j denote total U.S. exports to, and imports from,
country j; the superscript "e" pertains to adjusted values.

$$IIT_{ji} = 1 - \frac{|X_{ji}^e - M_{ji}^e|}{X_{ji}^e + X_{ji}^e} = 1 - \frac{|\frac{X_{ji}}{X_j} - \frac{M_{ji}}{M_j}|}{(\frac{X_{ji}}{X_j} + \frac{M_{ji}}{M_j})} \tag{7.1}$$

where $X_{ji}^e = X_{ji} \frac{X_j + M_j}{2X_j}$ and $M_{ji}^e = M_{ji} \frac{X_j + M_j}{2M_j}$

The index of intra-industry trade takes values from 0 to 1 as the extent
of intra-industry trade increases. However, if estimation is made by
using a linear or loglinear function, the predicted values may exceed one;
they may also be negative if the regression equation is linear. In turn,

---

1/ For reasons first explained in Balassa (1979), a modified form of the
    Aquino (1978) adjustment has been used in defining the index of intra-
    industry trade.

with a logistic function or its logit transformation, the predicted values are always between 0 and 1.

A linear regression equation was estimated by ordinary least squares by the authors cited in Chapter 4, except for Pagoulatos and Sorensen (1975) who estimated a loglinear function, and Loertscher and Wolter (1980) who estimated a logit transformation by weighted least squares, so as to eliminate a potential source of heteroscedascity. The latter method was also used by Caves (1981).

The adjustment for heteroscedasticity is justified by these authors by reference to the minimum chi-square estimation of the logit model in the case of multiple observations. Following Maddala (1983, section 2.8), suppose IIT_{ji} in equation (7.2) is obtained as m_{ji}/n_{ji}, where n_{ji} is the number of observations corresponding to z_{ji} and m_{ji} the number "successes," i.e. of occurrences of some event; then if n_{ji} is large, the residual u_{ji} of equation (7.2) has approximately a variance of $\sigma^2 W_{ji}^2$, where $W_{ji}^2 = 1/n_{ji} \, IIT_{ji}(1-IIT_{ji})$. In the equation, z_{ji} is the vector of

$$\ln \frac{IIT_{ji}}{1-IIT_{ji}} = \beta' z_{ji} + u_{ji} \tag{7.2}$$

explanatory variables (including a constant), β the corresponding vector of coefficients, j refers to country characteristics and i pertains to industry characteristics.

The correct estimation procedure involves multiplying the dependent variable as well as each of the explanatory variables by the weighting factor $\sqrt{n_{ji} \, IIT_{ji}(1-IIT_{ji})}$, with ordinary least squares applied to the transformed variables. Loerstcher and Wolter appropriately weighted the

explanatory variables but neglected to weight the dependent variable. [1]
In turn, as noted by Bergstrand (1983), Caves divided rather than
multiplied the dependent and the explanatory variables by the adjustment
factor. [2]

The experience of the present study indicates that the use of the wrong
adjustment procedure may affect the results to a considerable extent.
Thus, dividing instead of multiplying the dependent and the explanatory
variables by the adjustment factor $\overline{IIT_{ji}(1-IIT_{ji})}$ reduces the number
of variables with a t-value of 2.5 or higher from fourteen to two. Also,
the coefficient of determination declines from 0.87 to 0.10. [3]

Further questions arise about the appropriateness of the adjustment
procedure. The definition of IIT_{ji} given in formula (7.1) does not
match its interpretation as a proportion m_{ji}/n_{ji} of "successes" in a
sequence of n_{ji} independent Bernouilli trials that is required to
justify this kind of adjustment for heteroscedasticity. Nor do Loerstcher
and Wolter, Caves, and Bergstrand provide a justification for such an
interpretation, although they use the adjustment procedure. At the same
time, estimation in the present case does not furnish evidence of this
kind of heteroscedasticity.

Also, while the logit transformation has the advantage of ensuring that

---

1/ As explained in the Technical Appendix to Chapter 6, this error is
    likely to distort their results considerably. Note that these authors
    assumed that n_{ji} = 1 in the adjustment factor, which means that they
    could not have interpreted the index of intra-industry trade in terms
    of the number of occurrences of a certain outcome in a certain number
    of trials.

2/ Caves uses the total size of the U.S. industry, measured by value
    added, instead of n_{ji}, in the adjustment factor.

3/ It is not suggested, however, that similar differences would arise in
    regard to Caves' results. The more extreme values of IIT_{ji} there are
    in the sample, the more the results can be expected to differ, not
    only between incorrect or correct weighted least squares, but even
    between any of these methods and ordinary least squares applied to
    (7.2). The range of Caves' data is 0.25 to 0.82 (with only 7
    observations outside the range .40 to .82), while in the present study
    the range is 0.01 to 0.99.

predicted values are within the appropriate range, it has the disadvantage of excluding all observations where the index of intra-industry trade takes values of 0 or 1. Although none of the indices are equal to one in the present case, nearly one-third of the observations equal zero, indicating the absence of intra-industry trade. Zero observations occur if there are exports of commodity i to country j but there are no corresponding imports (27.1 percent of the observations in the U.S. case) or if there are imports but no exports (4.3 percent). [1]

Given the need to include zero observations -- representing the absence of intra-industry trade -- in an econometric investigation of this trade, and the importance of these observations in the data, an estimating procedure had to be sought that can handle zero observations. Such a procedure is non-linear least squares estimation, which gives predicted values from 0 to 1 for the index of intra-industry trade. This procedure has the further advantage that it avoids the problems related to the adjustment procedure employed in conjunction with weighted least squares.

Correspondingly, in the present investigation use has been made of the non-linear least squares method. This has involved the estimation of equation (7.3). Estimates have been made including as well as excluding zero observations, so as to permit comparisons with the results obtained by weighted least squares.

$$IIT_{ji} = 1 \ / \ (1+e^{-\beta'z_{ji}}) + \varepsilon_{ji} \qquad (7.3)$$

7.3 Empirical Results for the United States

Table 7.1 shows the results obtained by weighted least squares and by nonlinear least squares, excluding as well as including zero observations. It is apparent that the t-values for all the variables rise and the number of statistically significant results increases to a

---

[1] Note that in cases where there are neither exports nor imports (5.9 percent of the observations) the index of intra-industry trade is not defined, and the observations have been excluded from the statistical analysis.

Table 7.1

The Determinants of Intra-Industry Specialization in U.S. Trade

(regression coefficients, with t-values in parenthesis)

Logit Analysis with

	Weighted Least Squares with correct adjustment for heteroscedasticity		Nonlinear Least Square Estimates excluding zero observations		including zero observations	
Constant	-0.207	(1.48)	-0.202	(1.45)	-0.138	(1.07)
Product differentiation (PD)	0.174	(2.63)	0.243	(3.63)	0.443	(6.95)
Marketing (MKT)	0.777	(0.88)	1.556	(0.92)	5.839	(6.80)
Plant economies of scale (ECSC)	-1.125	(1.22)	-1.217	(1.39)	-4.369	(4.71)
Concentration ratio (IACR)	-1.033	(2.38)	-1.194	(2.67)	-3.665	(6.45)
Offshore assembly (OAP)	0.277	(2.16)	0.254	(1.98)	0.543	(4.30)
Income inequality (INEQ Y/P)	-0.130	(1.05)	-0.584	(4.63)	-1.811	(12.69)
Size inequality (INEQY)	-0.222	(2.01)	-0.462	(4.18)	-0.905	(8.47)
Trade orientation (ATO)	0.144	(2.67)	0.182	(3.43)	0.478	(8.82)
Distance (ln D)	-0.484	(4.32)	-0.723	(6.41)	-1.115	(9.36)
$\bar{R}^2$	0.0995		0.5598		0.4767	
$\hat{\sigma}$	0.4654		0.2973		0.2635	
N	3191		3191		4930	

considerable extent if nonlinear rather than weighted least squares estimation is used.

This comparison has been made by excluding from estimation by nonlinear least squares the zero observations that are ipso facto excluded under weighted least squares estimation. In the majority of cases, further improvements occur if zero observations are also included in estimation by nonlinear least squares.

The theoretically more appropriate nonlinear least squares estimation thus gives statistically superior results than weighted least squares. At the same time, one needs to include in the estimation the zero observations that indicate the absence of intra-industry trade. Correspondingly, the following discussion is limited to estimates obtained by applying nonlinear least squares estimation to all (zero as well as non-zero) observations.

Among the industry variables, the Hufbauer measure of product differentiation has the expected positive sign and a t-value of 7.0 while the marketing variable that has a positive coefficient, with a t-value of 6.8. The suggested interpretation of these results is that intra-industry trade between the United States and any of its partners increases with the extent of product differentiation.

The plant economies of scale variable is negatively correlated with the extent of intra-industry trade, with a t-value of 4.7. This is the expected result as the variable is taken to reflect the extent of product standardization. A negative coefficient, with a t-value of 6.5, is also obtained for the industrial concentration variable that is considered to be another indicator of product standardization. Finally, the offshore assembly variable has the expected positive sign and a t-value of 4.6.

Among country variables, both the income inequality and the size inequality variables have the expected negative signs, with t-values of 12.7 and 8.5, respectively. Thus, the assumed negative relationship between differences in income levels and market size on the one hand, and the extent of intra-industry trade, on the other, is confirmed by the empirical results.

Furthermore, as expected, trade orientation is positively correlated with the extent of intra-industry trade while a negative correlation is obtained with respect to distance. Both of these variables are highly significant statistically, with t-values of 8.8 and 9.4, respectively.

The coefficient of determination of the regression equation estimated by non-linear least squares [1] with the inclusion of zero observations is 0.48. Thus, approximately one-half of the variation in the extent of intra-industry trade is explained by the industry and country variables utilized in the estimation. The inclusion of zero observations has reduced the adjusted R^2 that was 0.57 in the case when these observations were excluded but it has also decreased the value of $\hat{\sigma}$, the residual standard deviation, from 0.30 to 0.26. At the same time, the results compare favorably with an $\hat{\sigma}$ value 0.47 obtained in estimation by weighted least squares. [2]

7.4   Empirical Results for the Other Major Industrial Countries

Table 7.2 reports the results for the other major industrial countries: France, Germany, the United Kingdom, and Japan. Given the superiority of nonlinear least-squares estimation, inclusive of zero observations, only the results obtained by this estimation procedure are reported in the table.

It should be noted at the outset that one cannot expect a high degree of statistical significance from the industry variables which have been estimated for the United States and "transplanted" to the other countries. This problem does not arise, however, in regard to the country variables, which are estimated pairwise for each country and its trading

---

[1] On the definition of the coefficient of determination, see the Technical Appendix to Chapter 5.

[2] As explained in the Technical Appendix to Chapter 5, the residual standard deviation is a goodness of fit measure that is comparable between different methods of estimation.

Table 7.2

The Determinants of Intra-Industry Specialization

in the Trade of Selected Countries

(regression coefficients, with t-values in parenthesis)

Nonlinear Least Squares, including zero observations

	France		Germany		United Kingdom		Japan	
Constant	2.970	(13.77)	3.764	(19.24)	2.355	(7.58)	3.027	(3.08)
Product differentiation (PD)	0.055	(0.71)	0.058	(0.83)	0.131	(1.44)	0.009	(0.09)
Marketing (MKT)	0.084	(0.08)	0.071	(0.07)	5.342	(4.04)	8.202	(6.08)
Plant Economies of Scale								
(ECSC)	−3.663	(3.80)	−2.915	(3.40)	−0.035	(0.03)	0.281	(0.23)
Concentration Ratio (IACR)	−2.121	(4.64)	−1.105	(3.13)	−8.469	(7.13)	−7.051	(5.25)
Offshore Assembly (OAP)	0.312	(2.21)	0.352	(2.77)	1.137	(6.33)	1.299	(6.14)
Income Inequality (INEQ Y/P)	−1.757	(9.45)	−1.150	(7.33)	−1.294	(6.19)	−2.292	(7.60)
Size Inequality (INEQY)	−1.603	(16.14)	−1.371	(15.52)	−0.572	(5.20)	−2.088	(12.55)
Trade Orientation (ATO)	0.596	(10.21)	0.686	(11.35)	0.617	(9.53)	0.269	(2.86)
Distance (ln D)	−0.412	(15.67)	−0.577	(24.27)	−0.536	(13.11)	−0.453	(4.70)
$\bar{R}^2$	0.5546		0.5656		0.3990		0.3100	
$\hat{\sigma}$	0.2472		0.2453		0.2387		0.2265	
N	3951		4701		3231		3100	

partners.

The empirical results bear out these expectations. Thus, while -- with one exception -- the industry variables have the expected sign, their level of statistical significance varies. At the same time, all country variables have the expected sign and a high level of statistical significance.

The Hufbauer product differentiation and the marketing variables have the expected positive sign. However, the former does not reach the 10 percent level of significance for any of the four countries. And while the latter is significant at the 1 percent level for the United Kingdom and Japan, it does not meet the significance test for France and Germany.

The plant economies of scale and industrial concentration variables have the expected negative sign, except for the former in the case of Japan. The industrial concentration variable is significant at the 1 percent level for all four countries; this is also the case in regard to the plant economies of scale variable for France and Germany.

The offshore assembly variable has the expected positive sign and it is statistically significant at the 1 percent level in all four countries. Apart from industrial concentration, then, this industry variable has given uniformly the most satisfactory results.

Among the country variables, both the income inequality and the size inequality variables have the expected negative sign and are statistically significant at the 1 percent level for all four countries. Also, the expected positive correlation obtains for trade orientation variable and the expected negative correlation for the distance variable; all the results are highly significant statistically.

Finally, the coefficient of determination is 0.55 for France and 0.57 for Germany, only slightly below the U.S. level. It is, however, only 0.40 for the United Kingdom and 0.31 for Japan.

7.5 Summary

This chapter set out to explain the extent of intra-industry specialization in United States trade with 37 countries exporting manufactured goods in 167 manufacturing industries. This has been done by testing hypotheses derived from international trade theory in regard to the inter-industry and intercountry determinants of the extent of intra-industry trade.

Utilizing data on U.S. trade with 37 trading partners in individual industries, it has been found that the extent of intra-industry trade is positively correlated with product differentiation, marketing costs, and offshore procurement, and it is negatively correlated with economies of scale and industrial concentration. These results confirm the theoretical expectations and the regression coefficients are statistically significant at the 1 percent level. It is recalled that the marketing costs variable also represents product differentiation while the economies of scale and industrial concentration variables reflect the extent of product standardization.

It has further been shown that the extent of intra-industry specialization in U.S. trade with individual countries is positively correlated with the extent of trade orientation in these countries and negatively correlated with inequalities in per capita incomes and total GNP and with distance between the U.S. and the individual countries. Again, the results conform to theoretical expectations and the regression coefficients are statistically significant at least at the 10 percent level.

These results have been obtained by nonlinear least squares estimation that is superior to weighted least squares owing to the inclusion of zero observations, indicating the absence of intra-industry trade, which account for nearly one-third of the observations as well as by reason of the problems associated with the adjustment procedure involved in estimation by weighted least square. At the same time, considering the fact that the large number of zero observations reduce the coefficient of determination, and considerable errors are associated with the measurement of several of the variables, the explanatory power of the regression equation may be considered to be rather high.

Estimates have further been made for the trade of the other major
industrial countries, France, Germany, the United Kingdom and Japan.
While the use of U.S. data in the estimation has reduced the statistical
significance of the estimates obtained by the use of the industry
variables, the hypotheses put forward in regard to these variables are
generally supported by the results. Also, the country variables show a
high degree of statistical significance as beforehand. Finally, one-third
to one-half of the variations in the extent of intra-industry trade is
explained by the industry and country variables introduced in the
estimation.

Chapter 8

INTRA-INDUSTRY SPECIALIZATION
IN A MULTI-COUNTRY AND MULTI-INDUSTRIAL MODEL

8.1 Introduction

Chapter 6 examined the determinants of intra-industry specialization in manufactured goods in bilateral trade, with reference to country characteristics affecting this trade. Chapter 7 investigated the effects on intra-industry specialization of industry as well as country characteristics in the trade of selected countries. In this chapter, the determinants of intra-industry specialization are analyzed in the trade of every country with every other country in each industry category, with respect to country as well as industry characteristics.

Country characteristics pertain to pairs of countries; they include common (average per capita income, income differences, average country size, size differences, distance, common borders, and average trade orientation) and specific (participation in economic integration schemes and common language) country characteristics. Industry characteristics pertain to individual industries; they include product differentiation, marketing costs, scale economies, industrial concentration, and offshore assembly.

The study includes 38 countries whose manufactured exports exceeded $300 million, and accounted for at least 18 percent of their total merchandise exports, in 1979. Apart from trade among all the countries concerned, estimates have been made for trade among developed countries, among developing countries, between developed and developing countries, and among European countries. The investigation covers 167 industry categories in the manufacturing sector as defined by the United States

Standard Industrial Classification (SIC), omitting natural resource products whose manufacture is importantly affected by the availability of natural resources in a particular country (cf. Chapter 4).

Section 8.2 describes the methodology utilised. Section 8.3 lists the hypotheses to be tested and the variables used in empirical testing. Section 8.4 provides the empirical results obtained by introducing country and industry characteristics simultaneously. Section 8.5 reports the results obtained by introducing these variables separately and adding interaction terms for selected country and industry characteristics.

8.2   The Methodology Applied

The index of intra-industry trade, IIT_{jki} , has been defined as in (8.1), where X^e_{jki} and M^e_{jki} stand for the adjusted exports and imports of industry i in trade between countries j and k. The formula makes an adjustment for imbalance in total trade between countries j and k, when X_{jk} and M_{jk} represent the total exports and imports of country j in trade with country k. [1] The index takes values from 0 to 1 as the extent of intra-industry trade increases.

$$IIT_{jki} = 1 - \frac{|X^e_{jki} - M^e_{jki}|}{X^e_{jki} + M^e_{jki}} = 1 - \frac{\left|\dfrac{X_{jki}}{X_{jk}} - \dfrac{M_{jki}}{M_{jk}}\right|}{\dfrac{X_{jki}}{X_{jk}} + \dfrac{M_{jki}}{M_{jk}}} \qquad (8.1)$$

In the regression equations explaining intercountry and inter-industry differences in the extent of intra-industry trade, IIT_{jki} has been used as the dependent variable while the explanatory variables include the country and industry characteristics referred to above. The next few paragraphs discuss some considerations determining the choice of the functional form utilised in the estimation.

---

[1] While Aquino (1978) made an adjustment for the imbalance in trade in manufactured goods, the present study follows Balassa (1979) in adjusting for the imbalance in total trade, so as to allow for inter-industry specialisation between primary and manufactured goods that is of particular importance in trade between developed and developing countries.

A linear or loglinear equation may give predicted values that lie outside the 0 to 1 range. While a logistic function does not have this shortcoming, its logit transformation [1] cannot handle values of 0 and 1. Although values of 1 (representing complete intra-industry specialisation) do not occur in the sample, values of 0 (representing complete inter-industry specialisation) are of importance.

In trade among all the countries concerned, there are 106,856 potential observations. [2] IIT_{jki} is, however, not defined in 41 percent of the cases, because $X_{jki} = M_{jki} = 0$; i.e. no trade takes place in a particular industry category between two particular countries. Among the remaining 62,770 observations, 51 percent are equal to 0, because either X_{jki} or M_{jki} is zero; i.e. there is complete inter-industry specialisation.

Given the importance of zero observations, we have used the nonlinear least squares estimation of the logistic function to handle such observations. We have thus estimated (8.2), where b is the vector of the regression coefficients, z_{jki} is the vector of the explanatory variables, and ε_{jki} is a random disturbance term. The estimation has been done by decomposing $b'z_{jki}$ as shown in (8.3), where b^C and b^I are vectors of the regression coefficients of the explanatory variables, z_{jk}^C is the vector of characteristics of countries j and k and z_i is the vector of industry characteristics. [3]

$$IIT_{jki} = \frac{1}{1+\exp(-b'z_{jki})} + \varepsilon_{jki} \qquad (8.2)$$

---

[1] $\ln(IIT_{jki}/1-IIT_{jki}) = b'z_{jki} + u_{jki}$

[2] There are 38 countries trading with 37 countries in 152 commodity categories, but one-half of the observations are eliminated since $IIT_{jki} = IIT_{kji}$. (Some of the 167 commodity categories had to be dropped for lack of data for several industry characteristics at the required level of disaggregation.)

[3] On the definition of country and industry characteristics for pairs of countries, see Section 8.3.

$$b' z_{jki} = b_o + b^{C'} z_{jk}^C + b^{I'} z_i \qquad\qquad (8.3)$$

While none of the individual terms in (8.3) includes both the country and the industry dimensions of the variation of the dependent variable IIT_{jki} , they are both incorporated in the entire function. This means that the effects of country characteristics on the index of intra-industry specialisation are assumed to be invariant across industries and the effects of industry characteristics on the index of intra-industry specialisation are assumed to be invariant across country pairs.

It may be asked if it is necessary to include country and industry characteristics in a single equation rather than making separate estimates using only one of the two sets of characteristics. The answer to this question turns on whether the estimated coefficients differ as between the alternative formulations. This issue is considered below.

A second question is whether there is an interaction between country and industry characteristics. While the introduction of all possible pairs of country and industry characteristics, involving the estimation of a very large number of regression coefficients, would be computationally difficult, an attempt has been made to introduce interaction terms in cases when these can be regarded as economically meaningful. [1]

8.3   The Hypotheses to be Tested

In what follows, we state the hypotheses that have been tested in the present investigation and define the explanatory variables utilised in the estimation. This has been done on the basis of the literature reviewed in Chapter 4.

---

[1]   No attempt has been made, however, to examine interactions between pairs of country characteristics or pairs of industry characteristics.

Country Characteristics

It is hypothesised that the extent of intra-industry trade between any pair of countries will be

(1) positively correlated with their average per capita income, representing the extent of demand for differentiated products;

(2) negatively correlated with the differences between their per capita income, representing differences in their demand structures and/or differences in their resource endowments;

(3) positively correlated with their average size, indicating the possibilities for increasing the variety of differentiated products manufactured under economies of scale; and

(4) negatively correlated with the difference between their size, indicating differences in their ability to manufacture differentiated products.

In testing hypotheses (1) to (4), per capita income has been represented by GNP per head and country size by GNP. [1/] Instead of taking the absolute values of intercountry differences in per capita income and size, however, we have used a measure indicating relative differences that takes values between 0 and 1 (cf. Chapter 4).

It is hypothesised that the extent of intra-industry trade between any pair of countries will be

(5) negatively correlated with the distance between them, representing the availability and the cost of information necessary for trading differentiated products; and

(6) positively correlated with the existence of common borders,

---

[1/] While the domestic consumption of manufactured goods would have been a more appropriate measure of the size of the domestic market for these products, the necessary data are not available for some countries and are subject to considerable error in regard to others. At the same time, from available information it appears that the consumption of manufactured goods and the gross national product are highly correlated.

indicating the possibilities for intra-industry trade in response
to locational advantages.

In testing hypothesis (5), distance has been measured in terms of miles
between the centers of geographical gravity for each pair of countries.
In turn, the existence of common borders (hypothesis 6) has been
represented by a dummy variable.

It is hypothesised that the extent of intra-industry trade between any
pair of countries will be

   (7) negatively correlated with their average level of trade barriers,
        indicating the possibilities for intra-industry specialisation
        under trade liberalisation; and
   (8) positively correlated with participation in regional integration
        schemes, including the European Common Market, the European Free
        Trade Association and the Latin American Free Trade Association,
        indicating the possibilities of intra-industry trade in the
        framework of regional integration schemes.

Estimates of tariff levels are not available for a number of countries and
the tariff equivalent of quantitative import restrictions is not known
with any confidence for others.   An indicator of trade orientation has
therefore been used to represent the extent of trade restrictions for the
individual countries.   Trade orientation has been defined in terms of
percentage deviations of actual from hypothetical values of per capita
exports, with positive (negative) deviations taken to represent a low
(high) degree of restrictiveness.   This has been done by the use of the
procedure described in Chapter 2.

For any pair of countries, the sum of their trade orientation index has
been introduced in the estimating equations to test the hypothesis that
the extent of intra-industry trade is positively correlated with trade
orientation.   In turn, dummy variables have been introduced to represent
participation in the European Common Market (EEC), the European Free Trade
Association (EFTA), and the Latin American Free Trade Area (LAFTA) by the
trading partners.

It is hypothesised that the extent of intra-industry trade between any pair of countries will be

(9) positively correlated with the use of a common language, including English, French, Spanish, German, Portuguese, and Scandinavian (Danish, Norwegian, Swedish, and Finnish).

Hypothesis (9) has been tested by introducing dummy variables for each of these languages for any pair of countries where the same language is spoken.

Industry Characteristics

It is hypothesised that the extent of intra-industry trade in the products of a particular industry will be

(10) positively correlated with the degree of product differentiation; and

(11) negatively correlated with the degree of product standardisation.

Hypothesis (10) has been tested by defining product differentiation in terms of (a) the coefficient of variation of export unit values, and (b) marketing expenditures expressed as a percentage of total costs.

Hypothesis (11) has been tested by defining product standardisation in terms of (a) the extent of plant economies of scale, measured by dividing the ratio of the average size of shipments of the largest plants in U.S. industry, (accounting for approximately one-half of industry shipment) to total industry shipment, by the ratio of value added per worker in smaller plants (again accounting for one-half of industry shipments) to value added per worker in larger plants and (b) the extent of industry concentration, measured by dividing the share of the largest four firms in an industry's output, by the share of imports in industry output.

It is hypothesised that the extent of intra-industry trade in the products of the particular industry will be

(12) positively correlated with offshore assembly that encourages the
international division of labor, involving vertical
specialisation; it has been tested by utilising data on the
relative importance of offshore assembly in individual industries
in the United States.

8.4   The Empirical Results

The estimates reported in Table 8.1 relate to trade in manufactured goods
in 1971 [1] among all the countries concerned (Column 1), among developed
countries (Column 2), among developing countries (Column 3), between
developed and developing countries (Column 4), and among European
countries (Column 5).

The empirical results in column 1 of Table 8.1 support the hypotheses put
forward in regard to the effects of common country characteristics on
intra-industry trade. As expected, the extent of intra-industry trade is
positively correlated with average per capita incomes (AY/P), average
country size (AY), average trade orientation (ATO), and the existence of a
common border (BORDER), and it is negatively correlated with income
differences (INEQY/P), difference in country size (INEQY), and distance
(D). All the variables are highly significant statistically.

Among specific country characteristics, the EEC, EFTA, and LAFTA dummy
variables have the expected positive sign and are highly significant
statistically. In turn, the regression coefficients of the language dummy
variables have a positive sign, but their level of statistical
significance varies. The English, French, and German language variables
are significant at the 1 percent level, the Portuguese language variable
at the 5 percent level, while the Spanish and Scandinavian language
variables are not significant at even the 10 percent level.

---

[1] While the calculations refer to 1971, data for manufactured exports in
the year 1979 have been used as a benchmark for the choice of the
countries for the present investigation, so as to include countries
that have shown a potential to export manufactured goods.

Table 8.1

Estimation of Intra-Industry Trade
in a Multi-Country and Multi-Industry Framework
(regression coefficients, with t-values in parenthesis)

	(1)		(2)		(3)		(4)		(5)	
Constant	1.384	(16.05)	1.716	(7.40)	-2.272	(3.81)	1.632	(11.89)	0.594	(3.00)
ln AY/P	0.686	(29.96)	0.431	(5.91)	0.785	(7.97)	0.692	(13.41)	0.761	(16.97)
INEQY/P	-1.044	(20.96)	0.200	(0.71)	-0.353	(1.90)	-0.746	(11.66)	-0.923	(8.10)
ln AY	0.349	(36.48)	0.358	(17.29)	-0.431	(4.25)	0.433	(25.09)	0.286	(10.86)
INEQY	-0.863	(27.03)	-0.825	(14.57)	0.995	(3.08)	-1.151	(18.52)	-1.156	(18.98)
ATO	0.452	(32.68)	0.364	(5.28)	0.253	(7.84)	0.533	(26.48)	0.698	(11.35)
ln D	-0.372	(49.16)	-0.357	(26.15)	-0.397	(10.66)	-0.395	(29.44)	-0.265	(11.96)
BORDER	0.302	(11.91)	0.273	(7.77)	0.612	(4.16)	0.549	(10.54)	0.321	(9.86)
EEC	0.161	(4.95)	0.146	(3.50)					0.074	(1.84)
EFTA	0.309	(12.69)	0.295	(9.10)			0.354	(6.25)	0.177	(5.65)
LAFTA	0.596	(4.37)			1.366	(7.79)				
ENGLISH	0.087	(3.04)	-0.083	(1.80)	0.607	(8.22)	0.089	(1.94)	0.832	(8.10)
FRENCH	0.197	(2.73)	0.391	(3.58)	-0.440	(0.56)	0.028	(0.20)	0.483	(5.57)
SPANISH	0.056	(0.29)			1.243	(4.77)				
GERMAN	0.268	(5.11)	0.308	(4.72)					0.293	(4.70)
PORT.	0.624	(2.02)			0.976	(3.63)				
SCAND.	0.052	(1.24)	0.101	(1.87)					0.102	(1.93)
PD	0.288	(14.06)	0.378	(12.60)	0.264	(3.21)	0.039	(1.15)	0.316	(10.08)
MKT	3.550	(12.92)	2.965	(7.26)	3.670	(3.74)	6.790	(14.41)	2.127	(4.91)
ECSC	-2.156	(8.27)	-2.546	(6.80)	-0.457	(0.44)	-1.333	(3.11)	-2.341	(6.05)
IACR	-2.147	(15.16)	-1.387	(8.18)	-1.192	(2.08)	-8.845	(17.24)	-1.364	(7.91)
OAP	0.326	(8.49)	0.099	(1.79)	0.588	(3.69)	0.963	(14.26)	0.133	(2.31)
R^2	0.4425		0.5672		0.2265		0.2459		0.5825	
N	62,770		21,250		6,697		34,823		19,847	

Sources: For definition of the variables, see Table 4.1.

Notes: (13) Trade among developed and developing countries combined.
   (14) Trade among developed countries.
   (15) Trade among developing countries.
   (16) Trade between developed and developing countries.
   (17) Trade among European countries.

Among industry characteristics, the Hufbauer measure of product differentiation (PD) and the marketing variable (MKT) have the expected positive sign and are highly significant statistically. Also, as expected, the economies of scale (ECSC) and the industrial concentration (IACR) variables are negatively correlated with the extent of intra-industry trade; they are highly significant statistically. Finally, the offshore assembly variable (OAP) has the expected positive sign and is highly significant statistically.

The results for the developed country group reported in Column 2 of Table 8.1 confirm the conclusions obtained for the entire group of countries as regards common country characteristics, the only exception being the income difference variable whose coefficient does not differ significantly from 0.[1] This exception may be explained by the fact that the relatively small differences in per capita incomes among developed countries tend to make their demand structure similar. Correspondingly, one may not expect large variations to occur in the extent of intra-industry trade as a function of income differences.

The stated hypotheses are also confirmed in regard to participation in integration arrangements and the responsiveness of intra-industry trade to having French and German as common languages among the developed countries. However, the English language variable has the incorrect sign, possibly reflecting the effect of longstanding economic separation among the countries concerned. Finally, the level of statistical significance approached 10 percent for the Scandinavian language in the developed country group.

All product differentiation and product standardisation variables continue to be highly significant in the developed country group. The offshore procurement variable is significant at the 10 percent level.

The results obtained for intra-industry trade among developing countries,

---

[1] The estimated results are shown in Column 2 of Table 8.1, omitting the dummy variables for LAFTA and for the Spanish and Portuguese languages, which are not relevant for trade among developed countries.

reported in Column 3 of Table 8.1, [1/] also confirm the stated hypotheses about average income levels, income differences, trade orientation, distance, and border trade. All the coefficients are highly significant statistically, except for the income difference variable (which is significant at the 5 percent level). The explanation for this result is similar to that adduced above in regard to trade among developed countries.

The hypotheses are not confirmed, however, for the average size and size difference variables; in fact, the signs are the opposite to those expected. In this connection, it should be noted that only about one-fourth of trade in manufactured goods among these countries is intra-industry trade and a few aberrant data may have influenced the outcome.

Among specific country characteristics, the LAFTA, English, Spanish, and Portuguese language variables are significant at the 1 percent level in the developing country group. The French language variable is not significantly different from zero, however, and has the wrong sign.

The offshore assembly variable is not relevant for trade among developing countries and has thus been excluded from the estimates. Of the remaining industry variables, product differentiation and marketing costs are statistically significant at the 1 percent level, while the industrial concentration variable is significant at the 10 percent level and the economies of scale variable approaches this level of significance.

All the variables representing common country characteristics are highly significant in intra-industry trade between developed and developing countries (Column 4 of Table 8.1). This conclusion also applies to the EFTA variable, while the English language variable is significant at the 10 percent level. The French language variable is not statistically significant, however.

1/ The EEC, EFTA, German and Scandinavian language variables are irrelevant in this context and have been excluded from the estimation.

Among industry characteristics, the marketing cost, industrial concentration, and offshore assembly variables are all highly significant statistically. The Hufbauer measure of product differentiation and the economies of scale variables are not statistically significant, however.

All the variables representing common country characteristics are significant at the 1 percent level in trade among European countries as well. The economic integration and the common language dummy variables also have the expected positive sign and are highly significant statistically, except that the EEC and Scandinavian language variables are significant only at the 10 percent level.

Both the Hufbauer measure of product differentiation and the marketing variable have the expected positive, and the economies of scale and industrial concentration variables the expected negative, sign and they are statistically significant at the 1 percent level. Finally, the offshore assembly variable has the expected positive sign and it is statistically significant at the 5 percent level.

On the whole, then, the hypotheses introduced in Section 8.3 have been successfully tested for intra-industry trade among various groups of countries. At the same time, the explanatory power of the regression for trade among all the countries concerned is relatively low, with a coefficient of determination of 0.44 in regard to intra-industry trade among all countries that export manufactured goods. This is hardly surprising given the great variability of intra-industry trade in individual industries between pairs of countries. In fact, the R^2 for intra-industry trade among the same group of countries is 0.87 if country averages for all industries are taken (Chapter 6).

The coefficient of determination is 0.57 for trade among developed countries and 0.58 for trade among European countries. These results appear to find their origin in the greater homogeneity of the economic structure of the developed country and the European country group. [1]

Estimates made for developed countries by Loertscher and Wolter (1980) have a much lower coefficient of determination (0.07). There may be two possible explanations for this result. First, Loertscher and Wolter estimated a logit equation that involves excluding zero observations; second, while these authors adjusted the explanatory variables for heteroscedascity, they failed to make this adjustment for the dependent variable. [2]

The coefficient of determination is 0.22 for intra-industry trade among developing countries and 0.25 for trade between developed and developing countries. In both cases, the heterogeneity of the sample and the relatively large proportion of zero observations appear to have reduced the explanatory power of the regression equations. [3] As far as trade among the developing countries is concerned, the prevalence of quantitative import restrictions may also reduce the extent of the correlation.

A further question concerns the relative importance of the individual variables in explaining variations in the extent of intra-industry trade. A full treatment of this question would have required an examination of all combinations of the explanatory variables, so as to take account of their joint contribution; this has not been attempted

---

[1] The proportion of observations for which intra-industry trade is equal to 0 is 22 percent in trade among developed countries, while it is 51 percent in trade among all countries. In the former case, the potential number of observations is 23256, but there are 2006 cases where no trade takes place.

[2] At the same time, as shown in Chapter 6, the values of the regression coefficients and their statistical significance are significantly affected by the use of the incorrect weighting procedure. Hence, little purpose would be served by comparing the results of this study with those of Loertscher and Wolter.

[3] The index of intra-industry specialization takes the value of 0 in 75 percent of the cases in trade among developing countries, and in 64 percent of the cases in trade between developed and developing countries.

here. In what follows we briefly report the increase of the coefficient of determination resulting from the addition of an explanatory variable, given the inclusion of all the other variables, in regard to intra-industry trade among all countries.

The results show that distance and average country size are the country characteristics that contribute the most to the explanatory power of the regression equations, followed by trade orientation, country size differences, and income differences. By contrast, introduction of the language variables adds little to the explanatory power of the equations.

Among industry characteristics, the industrial concentration variable has the greatest explanatory power, followed by the variables for marketing costs and offshore assembly. In turn, the variables for product differentiation and economies of scale do not appreciably increase the explanatory power of the regression equation.

8.5 Alternative Experiments

At this point it is appropriate to ask whether the results might differ if the country and industry variables were introduced separately, rather than simultaneously, into the estimation. This question has been addressed by decomposing equations (8.1) to (8.3) into equations containing only country characteristics and only industry characteristics, respectively. Table 8.2 reports the results obtained for intra-industry trade among all countries included in the investigation.

A comparison of Tables 8.1 and 8.2 shows that differences in the values of the regression coefficients for common country characteristics in no case attain 2 percent. The differences are larger for specific country characteristics, slightly exceeding 10 percent for the English and the Spanish language variables. At the same time, the statistical significance of the regression coefficients is hardly affected by the separate estimation of the two equations.

Different considerations apply to the industry variables. The regression coefficients of these variables show substantial differences. The

Table 8.2

Estimation of Intra-Industry Trade in a Multi-Country

and Multi-Industry Framework: Disaggregation of the Variables

(regression coefficients with t-values in parenthesis)

	Multi-country Model		Multi-industry model	
Constant	-1.746	(21.49)	-1.917	(50.00)
ln AY/P	0.677	(26.34)		
INEQY/P	-1.041	(20.52)		
ln AY	0.339	(35.29)		
INEQY	-0.859	(26.74)		
ATO	0.453	(32.49)		
ln D	-0.366	(48.08)		
BORDER	0.301	(11.90)		
EEC	0.150	(4.62)		
EFTA	0.303	(12.45)		
LAFTA	0.576	(4.13)		
ENGLISH	0.073	(2.56)		
FRENCH	0.204	(2.83)		
SPANISH	0.057	(0.29)		
GERMAN	0.264	(5.05)		
PORT.	0.541	(1.61)		
SCAND.	0.051	(1.20)		
PD			0.116	(4.98)
MKT			2.335	(7.62)
ECSC			-1.360	(4.49)
IACR			-1.697	(9.45)
OAP			0.401	(9.08)
R^2	0.4356		0.2697	
N	62770		62770	

Sources: See text.

Note: Trade among developed and developing countries combined.

Table 8.3

Estimation of Intra-Industry Trade in a Multi-Country and
Multi-Industry Framework, with Interaction Terms
(regression coefficients, with t-values in parenthesis)

Constant	0.265	(1.07)
ln AY/P	0.540	(8.19)
INEQY/P	-0.265	(1.74)
ln AY	0.354	(33.41)
INEQY	-0.608	(6.67)
ATO	0.449	(30.67)
ln D	-0.407	(51.29)
BORDER	0.305	(11.94)
EEC	0.081	(2.47)
EFTA	0.357	(14.57)
LAFTA	0.580	(4.12)
ENGLISH	0.035	(1.14)
FRENCH	0.278	(3.88)
SPANISH	0.063	(0.30)
GERMAN	0.338	(6.38)
PORT.	0.609	(1.80)
SCAND.	-0.166	(3.97)
PD	-0.117	(0.54)
MKT	3.517	(12.43)
ECSC	-0.876	(2.25)
IACR	-2.594	(7.42)
CAP	-0.410	(10.42)
ln AY/P x PD	0.152	(2.45)
INEQY/P x PD	-0.783	(5.24)
INEQY x PD	-0.124	(1.62)
ln AY x IACR	-0.233	(1.69)
INEQY X ECSC	-4.053	(4.30)

R^2	0.4413
N	62770

coefficient of the Hufbauer product differentiation variable and that of the economies of scale variable are more than one-half smaller and only the offshore assembly variable is larger. At the same time, the t-values of most of the regression coefficients are reduced, although they remain statistically significant at the 1 percent level, if industry characteristics are introduced separately rather than simultaneously with country characteristics in the estimation.

These results are confirmed by estimates made for the other four country groups. They thus indicate the appropriateness of introducing country and industry characteristics simultaneously in the estimating equation. At the same time, the results point to the desirability of examining the interaction between country and industry characteristics. This has been done by testing hypotheses that derive from those introduced earlier.

It is hypothesized that for any pair of countries

(13)   as per capita incomes and average country size rise and differences in incomes and country size fall, product differentiation will increase, and product standardization will reduce, the extent of intra-industry trade.

The estimated results are shown in Table 8.3 for intra-industry trade among all the countries covered in the investigation, with the exclusion of those coefficients of the interaction terms that are not significant at the 10 percent level. While the number of significant coefficients is relatively small, they support the above hypotheses with one exception.

It is observed that higher average per capita incomes and smaller differences in per capita income and size enhance the contribution of product differentiation (measured by the Hufbauer variable) to intra-industry trade. Also, the negative effects of product standardization, measured by the industrial concentration variable, on intra-industry trade are enhanced by increases in average country size. Contrary to expectations, however, larger country size differences appear to augment the negative effects of product standardization, measured by the economies of scale variables, on intra-industry trade.

While the results obtained by introducing interaction terms have an economic interpretation, their introduction affects the coefficient values of some of the country characteristics. However, the level of statistical significance declines for only two variables, per capita income differences and the EEC dummy. In turn, the Scandinavian language variable becomes significant at the 1 percent level, -- having not reached even a 10 percent level of significance without the introduction of interaction terms.

Among industry characteristics, the Hufbauer product differentiation variables loses its statistical significance when interaction terms are introduced in the estimating equation. The remaining variables, however, retain their sign and statistical significance and, except for the economies of scale variable, their coefficient values are little affected by the introduction of interaction terms.

8.6 Summary

This chapter has tested various hypotheses about the determinants of intra-industry specialization in manufactured goods, including common and specific country characteristics as well as industry characteristics. The study covers 38 countries exporting manufactured goods; calculations have been made for bilateral trade flows among all the 38 countries, among 18 developed countries, among 20 developing countries, between the 18 developed and the 20 developing countries, as well as among European countries.

The hypotheses put forward in the theoretical literature in regard to common country characteristics are generally confirmed by the empirical results. Thus, the extent of intra-industry trade is positively correlated with average income levels, average country size, trade orientation, and the existence of common borders and it is negatively correlated with income inequality, inequality in country size, and distance. [1]/ All the variables are highly significant statistically in the five calculations, except for the income inequality variable in trade among developed countries and among developing countries; in both cases income differences are smaller than in the entire country sample.

We also found that the extent of intra-industry trade and participation in the European Common Market, the European Free Trade Association, and the Latin American Free Trade Association are positively correlated, with all the coefficients being highly significant in the relevant equations. [2]/ Also, the language variables have the expected positive sign whenever they are statistically significant, which is the case in most instances.

The extent of intra-industry trade is expected to be positively correlated with product differentiation, represented by the Hufbauer measure and by marketing costs, and negatively correlated with product standardization, represented by economies of scale and by industrial concentration. All the regression coefficients have the expected sign and are generally significant statistically, the exceptions being the economies of scale variable in the case of trade among developing countries and between developed and developing countries; and the product differentiation variable in the case of trade between developed and developing countries. The offshore assembly variable also has the expected positive sign and it is highly significant statistically in all cases.

The estimates presented in this paper combine the intercountry and the inter-industry determinants of the extent of intra-industry trade. The explanatory power of the regression equation is greatest for trade among European and among developed countries, which have a relatively homogeneous economic structure and for which intra-industry trade represents an important proportion of total trade. However, the heterogeneity of the sample and the relatively large proportion of zero

---

1/ This conclusion does not apply to the size variables as far as trade among developing countries is concerned, however.

2/ The results indicate the importance of introducing industry characteristics in the investigation; in their absence, integration variables were not significant statistically (cf. Chapters 5 and 6).

observations appear to have reduced the explanatory power of the regressions for intra-industry trade among developing countries and between developed and developing countries.

It has further been shown that the simultaneous introduction of country and industry characteristics offers advantages over decomposition of the estimating equation into equations containing only country or industry characteristics.   Also, interaction terms between country and industry charcteristics have an economic interpretation whenever they are significant statistically, but their introduction modifies the results obtained in regard to several industry avariables.

Finally, the results of the equation estimated for all the countries under investigation indicate that the extent of intra-industry trade increases with the level of economic development, represented by per capita incomes.   Also, a comparison of the estimated equations for developed and developing countries show the changes in the determinants of intra-industry trade that occur as countries reach higher income levels.

Part III
THE DETERMINANTS OF INTER-INDUSTRY
AND INTRA-INDUSTRY TRADE
IN MANUFACTURED GOODS

Chapter 9

INTER-INDUSTRY AND INTRA-INDUSTRY SPECIALIZATION
IN MANUFACTURED GOODS

9.1 Introduction

Earlier chapters of this volume examined the determinants of inter-industry (Chapter 3) and intra-industry (Chapter 8) trade in manufactured goods in the framework of multi-country and multi-industry models. The former set out to explain the pattern of net trade (exports less imports or net exports) between pairs of countries in terms of interindustry differences in factor intensities and intercountry differences in factor endowments; the latter investigated the effects of country characteristics and industry characteristics on the extent of intra-industry specialization in trade between pairs of countries.

The present chapter combines the two approaches in the framework of a multi-country and multi-industry model. It analyses the determinants of gross trade between pairs of countries in individual industries. While net trade is affected by comparative advantage, gross trade is also influenced by the extent of intra-industry specialization, which increases exports as well as imports in bilateral trade. Furthermore, bilateral flows are affected by gravitational factors. [1]

In the model estimated in this paper, trade flows are measured as country j's exports of product i to country k. In the event of complete inter-

---

[1] Some of these factors were included as country characteristics affecting intra-industry specialization in Part II of this volume.

industry specialization, the gross exports of product i in trade between
any two countries will equal net exports, since a country will export but
not import a product in which it has a comparative advantage. In turn, in
the event of complete intra-industry specialization, net exports will be
zero. The joint occurrence of inter- and intra-industry specialization
will then make gross exports to exceed net exports, when trade between
pairs of countries is further influenced by gravitational variables.

The model thus includes three sets of variables affecting bilateral trade
in individual products (industries). They are: (a) variables affecting
comparative advantage, such as factor intensities and factor endowments;
(b) variables influencing intra-industry trade, such as country
characteristics and industry characteristics; and (c) variables
representing gravitational factors, such as distance and common language
and culture.

The investigation is limited to manufactured goods, where differences in
natural resource endowments do not enter into the determination of
comparative advantage. It covers 38 countries whose manufactured exports
exceeded $300 million, and accounted for at least 18 percent of their
total merchandise exports, in 1979. Apart from trade among all the
countries concerned, estimates have been made for trade among developed
countries, among developing countries, as well as between developed and
developing countries. Eighteen countries with per capita incomes of $2254
or higher in 1973 [1/] have been included in the developed, and twenty
countries with per capita incomes of $2031 or lower in 1973 [2/] in the

---

1/ In order of their per capita GNP, the countries in question are
    Switzerland, United States, Sweden, Denmark, Germany, Australia,
    Canada, Norway, France, Belgium, Netherlands, Japan, Finland, Austria,
    United Kingdom, Israel, Italy, and Ireland.

2/ In order of their per capita incomes, they are Spain, Singapore,
    Greece, Argentina, Hong Kong, Portugal, Yugoslavia, Mexico, Brazil,
    Taiwan, Malaysia, Tunisia, Korea, Morocco, Turkey, Egypt, Thailand,
    Philippines, India, and Pakistan.

developing, country group.

The investigation covers altogether 152 product categories in the
manufacturing sector as defined by the United States Standard Industrial
Classification (SIC), with the exclusion of natural resource products
whose manufacture is importantly affected by the availability of natural
resources in a particular country. [1] The classification scheme has been
established by merging 4-digit SIC categories in cases when the economic
characteristics of particular products have been judged to be very
similar.

Sections 9.2 and 9.3 describe the hypotheses to be tested in regard to
inter-industry and intra-industry specialization, respectively, and
provides the definitions for the relevant variables. Section 9.4 lists
the gravitational variables utilized. Section 9.5 provides information on
the econometric formulation and on the method of estimation. Finally,
Section 9.6 presents the results for trade among all the countries under
consideration while Section 9.7 contains the estimates for trade among
developed countries, among developing countries, and between developed and
developing countries and among European countries.

9.2 The Hypotheses to be Tested: Inter-Industry Trade

As explained in Chapter 3, comparative advantage is defined with respect
to industry and country characteristics.   Industry (product)

---

[1] The investigation excludes foods and beverages (SIC 20), tobacco (SIC
21), non-ferrous metals (SIC 333), as well as several 4-digit
categories covering textile waste, preserved wood, saw mill products,
prefabricated wood, veneer and plywood, wood pulp, dyeing and tanning
extracts, fertilizers, adhesives and gelatin, carbon black, petroleum
refining and products, asbestos and asphalt products, cement and
concrete, lime, gypsum products, cut stone products, and lapidary
work. It also excludes ordnance (SIC 19), for which comparable trade
data are not available.

characteristics refer to factor intensities, expressed as the value of physical capital per worker (p_i) and the value of human capital per worker (h_i) . In turn, country characteristics refer to the endowments of physical capital (G_j) and human capital (H_j), expressed in per capita terms.

In Chapter 3, the hypothesis was tested that, in trade between pairs of countries, relative capital abundance is associated with the net exports of capital intensive commodities. In the present chapter, this hypothesis will be tested in regard to gross exports. As in the earlier chapter, it will be tested for physical capital and for human capital, taken separately.

The estimating equation used in the Chapter 3 was derived utilizing a two-stage procedure. In the first stage, normalized net exports of product i from country j to country k (NNX_{jki}) [1]/ were regressed on physical (p_i) and human (h_i) capital intensities as in (1). [2]/ This was done for bilateral trade between countries j and k, such that j>k . In the second stage, the estimated coefficients, β_{jk}^p and β_{jk}^h were regressed, respectively, on the relative physical and human capital endowments of country j with respect to country k as in (2a) and (2b). [3]/

$$NNX_{jki} = \alpha_{jk} + \beta_{jk}^p \ln p_i + \beta_{jk}^h \ln h_i \qquad\qquad (9.1)$$

---

[1]/ Net exports of commodity i from country j to country k were normalized by dividing with the sum of exports and imports of commodity i in trade between countries j and k.

[2]/ In the following, we do not introduce residuals in the equations. For a discussion on these and the estimation method, see Chapter 3.

[3]/ Experiments were also made by including the human and the physical capital endowment variables in equations (9.2a) and (9.2b), respectively. The lack of statistical significance of the estimates was taken as an indication of the high degree of substitution between physical and human capital.

$$\beta^p_{jk} = a^p + b^p \ln \frac{G_j}{G_k} \qquad\qquad (9.2a)$$

$$\beta^h_{jk} = a^h + b^h \ln \frac{H_j}{H_k} \qquad\qquad (9.2b)$$

Substituting the right hand sides of these last two equations into the first yields equation (3) that was estimated in one step. The explanatory variables $\ln \frac{G_j}{G_k} \ln p_i$ and $\ln \frac{H_j}{H_k} \ln h_i$ are interaction terms between the relative endowment of j with respect to k in a given factor, and the intensity of use of this factor in the production of product i. In turn, the coefficients of $\ln p_i$ and $\ln h_i$ are the constants of the second stage equations.

$$NNX_{jki} = \alpha_{jk} + a^p \ln p_i + a^h \ln h_i + b^p \ln \frac{G_j}{G_k} \ln p_i + b^h \ln \frac{H_j}{H_k} \ln h_i \quad (9.3)$$

Data on the capital stock, employment, value added, and wages used in calculating physical and human capital intensities originate from the U.S. Census of Manufacturing and are averages for the years 1969 and 1970. Data on unskilled wages for the same period have been taken from the Monthly Labor Review, published by the U.S. Bureau of Labor Statistics; they pertain to the 2-digit industry group, thus involving the assumption that unskilled wages are the same within each 2-digit group.

Capital intensity has been defined in terms of stocks. Physical capital intensity has been equated to the value of the capital stock per worker while human capital intensity has been derived as the discounted value of the difference between the average wage and the unskilled wage using a 10 percent discount rate. [1]

---

[1] Apart from a stock measure of capital intensity, in Chapter 3 use has also been made of a flow measure, defined as non-wage value added per worker (physical capital) and the difference between the average wage and the unskilled wage (human capital). The two measures gave similar results and, in view of the high computer cost of estimating a large model, only the stock measure has been used here.

The trade data used in the investigation relate to 1971. They have been obtained from the GATT tapes. The commodity classification scheme employed has required the use of trade data down to the 5 digit level. In a few cases when 5-digit data were not available, they have been estimated from the 4-digit data on the basis of the worldwide composition of trade.

The sum of gross fixed investment over the seventeen year period between 1954 and 1970, estimated in constant prices and converted into U.S. dollars at 1967 exchange rates, has been used as a proxy for physical capital endowment for the countries concerned. Investment values have been assumed to depreciate at a rate of 4 percent a year, reflecting the obsolescence of capital, with capital equipment assumed to have a useful life of 17 years. The relevant information has been obtained from the World Bank economic and social data base, and the estimates have been expressed in per capita terms.

The Harbison-Myers index of education has been used as a proxy for human capital. The index is derived as the secondary school enrollment rate plus five times the university enrollment rate, both calculated in their respective age cohorts. It is a flow measure and estimates pertaining to 1965 have been utilized as an indicator of a country's general educational level, and thus its human capital base, in 1971.

9.3 The Hypotheses to be Tested: Intra-Industry Trade

As explained in Chapter 8, intra-industry specialization is affected by country and by industry characteristics. The former pertain to pairs of countries; they include average per capita incomes, income inequality, average country size, and size inequality. [1] The latter pertain to

---

1/ Some of the country characteristics included in the earlier paper (1987) will now appear as gravitational factors because they affect both inter-industry and intra-industry trade.

individual industries; they include product differentiation, marketing costs, plant economies of scale, industrial concentration, and offshore assembly.

Ceteris paribus, gross exports will be the greater, the greater is the extent of intra-industry trade. Correspondingly, this chapter will investigate the proposition that the variables which increase (reduce) the extent of intra-industry trade will also increase (reduce) gross exports. In the following, the individual hypotheses will be stated in a summary form; for details and references, see Chapter 4.

Country Characteristics

(1) Similarity in income levels has been said to contribute to intra-industry trade, which involves the exchange of differentiated products. Correspondingly, it will be hypothesized that the extent of intra-industry trade between any two countries is ˙negatively correlated with the difference between their income level. [1]

(2) Intra-industry trade has been said to increase with the rise of incomes that augments demand for differentiated products. It will thus be hypothesized that the extent of intra-industry trade between any two countries is positively correlated with their average income level.

(3) Similarity in country size has been said to contribute to intra-industry trade by equalizing conditions for the exportation of differentiated products manufactured under economies of scale. Accordingly, it will be hypothesized that the extent of intra-industry trade between any two countries is negatively correlated with the

---

[1] The income level of a country has been measured by its per capita GNP.

difference between their size. [1]

(4) Intra-industry trade has been said to increase with country size that permits increasing the number of differentiated products manufactured under economies of scale. It will, then, be hypothesized that the extent of intra-industry trade between any two countries is positively correlated with their average size.

Industry Characteristics

(1)   As noted above, intra-industry trade is associated with product differentiation. Correspondingly, it will be hypothesized that the extent of intra-industry trade is positively correlated with the degree of product differentiation. Two measures of product differentiation have been used in the present study:

> (a) the dispersion of prices (unit values) within each 7-digit SITC category; and
>
> (b) the ratio of marketing, planning, and support costs to total costs.

(2) Conversely, seasonal and border trade apart, intra-industry trade is not expected to occur in standardized products. It will thus be hypothesized that the extent of intra-industry trade is negatively correlated with the degree of product standardization. Two measures of product standardization has been used in this investigation:

> (a) plant economies of scale, measured by dividing the ratio of the average size of shipments of the larger plants in U.S. industry, accounting for approximately one-half of industry shipments, to total industry shipment by the ratio of value added per worker in the smaller establishments, again accounting for one-half of industry shipments, to

---

1/ The size of a country has been measured by its GNP.

value added per worker in the larger plants.

(b)   the concentration ratio, adjusted for the extent of import competition.

(3)   It has been said that offshore assembly provisions tend to lead to intra-industry trade by encouraging the international division of the production process.   Correspondingly, it will be hypothesized that the extent of intra-industry trade is positively correlated with the relative importance of offshore assembly, measured as the ratio of imports exempted from duties under offshore assembly provisions to total U.S. imports of the industry.

9.4 Gravitational Variables

Gravitational models have been used to explain bilateral trade in all products, taken together, by reference to variables that positively or negatively affect the extent of trade between pairs of countries without, however, introducing variables that determine inter-industry or intra-industry trade (Linneman, 1966).   In the present investigation, gravitational variables have been used in conjunction with variables affecting inter-industry and intra-industry specialization to explain bilateral trade in individual products (industries).   This has involved testing the following hypotheses: [1]

(1)   Ceteris paribus, bilateral trade will tend to decline with the cost of transportation.   Accordingly, it will be hypothesized that trade between any two countries is negatively correlated with the

---

[1]   It is customary to include in gravitational models a variable for country size to act as a scaling variable since trade tends to increase with the size of the trading partners.   Such a variable has not been utilized in the present study as the average GNP variable, described in conjunction with intra-industry trade, will act as a scaling variable.   This assumes symmetry as to the effects of the country size on trade between any two countries.

geographical distance between them, which is used as a proxy for transport costs.

(2)   Conversely, bilateral trade will be enhanced by the existence of common borders between any two countries. It will, then, be hypothesized that more trade occurs between countries that share a common border than between countries which do not have common borders, the existence of a common border is denoted by a dummy variable.

(3)   Bilateral trade will also be enhanced by the existence of low trade barriers in the countries in question. Thus, it will be hypothesized that more trade occurs between countries that have lower trade barriers than between countries with high barriers.

(4)   Participation in integration schemes will further contribute to trade among the participating countries. Correspondingly, it will be hypothesized that more trade occurs between any two countries which are members of a particular integration scheme than between countries which are not members. In the present investigation, dummy variables have been introduced for participation in the European Common Market, the European Free Trade Association, and the Latin Amerian Free Trade Association. (5)   Common language and cultural ties will also contribute to bilateral trade. It will thus be hypothesized that more trade occurs between any two countries with common language and cultural ties than between two countries without such ties. This hypothesis will be tested by introducing dummy variables for the English, French, Spanish, German, Portuguese, and Scandinavian language groups.

9.5   The Methodology Applied

To test the hypotheses stated in the Sections 9.1 to 9.4, we estimated equation (9.4) that incorporates the three sets of variables affecting the exports of commodity i from country j to country k, denoted by X_{jki} .

$$\ln X_{jki} = \beta_0 + \beta^{e'} z^e_{jki} + \beta^{a'} z^a_{jki} + \beta^{g'} z^g_{jk} + u_{jki} \qquad (9.4)$$

In the equation, z^e_{jki} is the vector of variables affecting inter-industry trade, i.e. the interaction terms described in Section 9.2. By definition, these interaction terms are assymetrical with respect to the country indices $(z^e_{jki} = -z^e_{kji})$. In turn, z^a_{jki} is the vector of variables influencing intra-industry trade, and Z_{jk}^g is the vector of gravitational variables. By construction, Z_{jki}^a and Z_{jk}^g are symmetrical (i.e. $Z_{jki}^a = Z_{kji}^a$ and $Z_{jk}^g = Z_{kj}^g$).

Since there are large number of zero or near to zero observations, estimation has been done by using the Tobit procedure; for details, refer e.g. to Maddala (1983). To simplify, suppose that there is only one explanatory variable in equation (4), say distance denoted D_{jk} . We have typically the following pattern of observations.

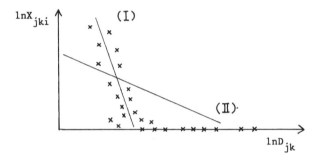

Neglecting the zero observations (crosses on the horizontal axis), entails losing the information that when distance becomes larger than a certain threshold, exports tend to become equal to zero. Application of ordinary least squares to the non-zero observations yielding (I), will bias the coefficients and will be inefficient statistically. Application of ordinary least squares to the complete sample (i.e. zero and non-zero observations), yielding (II), has the drawback of producing also biased estimates of the coefficient of $\ln D_{jk}$ and of the constant term, (II) being too flat as compared to (I). The Tobit procedure takes account of the zero observations, and will thus be efficient, without biasing the estimates of the regression coefficient. It produces an estimate of the true relationship that is interpretable for the zero and the non-zero observations, while OLS applied to the non-zero observations is not interpretable for the zero observations. In this case, the regression coefficient of $\ln D_{jk}$ represents the elasticity of exports with respect to distance, over the relevant ranges of $\ln X_{jk}$ and $\ln D_{jk}$. As shown by McDonald and Moffit (1980), the change in the expected value of $\ln X_{jk}$ resulting from a change in $\ln D_{jk}$ is not just the regression

Table 9.1: EXPLANATION OF TRADE IN MANUFACTURED GOODS AMONG THE MAJOR EXPORTERS OF THESE PRODUCTS

	Trade Among All Countries		Trade Among Developed Countries		Trade Among Developing Countries		Trade Between Developed and Developing Countries		Trade Among European Countries	
Constant	17.127	(119.34)	14.269	(37.98)	22.111	(33.53)	17.710	(74.33)	15.848	(49.21)
$\ln G_j/G_k$ $\ln p_i$	0.349	(73.21)	0.178	(11.32)	0.051	(2.50)	0.392	(61.66)	0.339	(34.29)
$\ln H_j/H_k$ $\ln h_i$	0.109	(15.40)	-0.126	(8.77)	0.233	(10.70)	0.123	(12.40)	0.183	(9.99)
INEQ Y/P	-1.647	(166.53)	-1.157	(2.58)	2.536	(10.23)	-2.115	(26.54)	-1.109	(9.48)
$\ln$ AY/P	2.293	(97.47)	1.712	(14.85)	2.041	(24.20)	2.100	(30.32)	2.361	(41.57)
INEQ Y	-3.095	(55.92)	-3.158	(32.98)	-2.310	(40.58)	-3.235	(37.08)	-2.876	(28.26)
$\ln$ AY	2.617	(166.53)	2.204	(64.74)	2.874	(31.18)	2.813	(115.57)	2.569	(62.10)
PD	1.054	(28.97)	1.204	(23.67)	0.727	(5.40)	1.121	(20.56)	0.766	(14.59)
MKT	21.792	(44.11)	20.000	(28.42)	29.494	(16.63)	23.127	(31.11)	14.290	(19.62)
ECSC	-11.259	(26.46)	-9.070	(15.94)	-14.974	(9.33)	-12.757	(19.95)	-11.567	(19.64)
IACR	-10.105	(54.55)	-8.929	(37.74)	-12.831	(15.87)	-11.196	(39.70)	-7.632	(31.05)
OAP	0.310	(4.70)					0.451	(4.56)		
$\ln$ D	-1.646	(126.60)	-1.242	(56.40)	-2.575	(49.65)	-1.651	(74.76)	1.349	(34.33)
BORDER	0.411	(6.11)	0.754	(10.66)	-0.050	(0.21)	1.116	(7.06)	0.725	(11.35)
ATO	1.937	(96.73)	2.100	(18.26)	2.393	(40.58)	2.137	(65.79)	1.479	(16.04)
EEC	0.556	(5.84)	0.790	(9.40)					0.511	(6.09)
EFTA	2.333	(37.98)	1.848	(31.01)			2.930	(24.75)	1.897	(35.55)
LAFTA	1.607	(5.66)			3.855	(8.16)				
ENGLISH	1.376	(37.47)	0.792	(10.94)	1.743	(11.16)	1.251	(19.19)	2.132	(9.78)
FRENCH	1.671	(13.37)	0.412	(1.91)	3.971	(6.51)	2.128	(13.00)	0.114	(0.53)
GERMAN	0.883	(5.37)	0.961	(7.08)					0.491	(3.69)
SCANDINAVIAN	0.600	(4.79)	0.709	(6.66)					0.584	(5.62)
SPANISH	1.863	(10.76)			5.018	(16.74)				
PORTUGUESE	1.423	(4.52)			3.303	(6.88)				
σ^2	20.479	(193.02)	12.252	(129.60)	6.657	(53.00)	24.29	(134.64)	12.330	(121.85)
N	213,712		46,512		57,760		109,440		46,512	
DEGREE OF CENSORING (In %)	57.65		20.33		85.88		49.46		N.A.	

Source: See Text

coefficient of ln D_{jk} when the Tobit specification is used: the change in the expected value of ln X_{jk} is equal to the change in ln X_{jk} if X_{jk} is positive, weighted by the probability that X_{jk} is positive, plus the change in the probability that X_{jk} is positive, weighted by the expected value of ln X_{jk} given that X_{jk} is positive. All these terms depend on the parameters β and σ^2, and on the value of the explanatory variables (ln D_{jk} here). Tobit procedure takes account of the zero observations to correct the bias.

9.6 Empirical Results for the Entire Country Group

Table 9.1 reports the results of estimation for trade (a) among all the 38 major exporters of manufactured goods, (b) among 18 developed countries, (c) among 20 developing countries, (d) between the developed and the developing countries covered by the investigation, and (e) among European countries. We will report first the results obtained for the trade of the entire group of countries, followed by a discussion of the results for the four country groupings.

The estimates for the entire group of countries included in the investigation confirm the hypotheses put forward earlier. All the regression coefficients have the expected sign and they are highly significant statistically.

To begin with, the results provide support to the Heckscher-Ohlin theory of international specialization, inasmuch as the relative factor intensity of trade is shown to be positively correlated with relative factor endowments; the more capital (labor) abundant is country j relative to country k, the more capital (labor) intensive will be its exports to that country. As shown by the positive signs of interaction terms ln G_j/G_k lnp_i and ln H_j/H_k ln h_i, this conclusion applies equally well to physical and to human capital.

The results further confirm the hypotheses put forward by various authors concerning the effects of country characteristics on intra-industry trade. Thus, it has been shown that trade flows between any two countries are the greater (a) the smaller are differences in their per capita incomes (INEQ Y/P), (b) the higher is their average per capita income (AY/P), (c) the smaller are differences in country size (INEQ Y), and (d) the greater is their average size (AY). [1]

Among industry characteristics, both measures of product differentiation -- price dispersion (PD) and marketing (MKT) -- are positively correlated with trade as it was hypothesized.   In turn, the expected negative correlation is obtained in regard to variables representing product standardization, including plant economies of scale (ECSC) and industrial concentration (IACR).   Finally, offshore assembly provisions (OAP) positively contribute to international trade flows as it was to be expected.

The results also confirm the relevance of gravitational factors for the pattern of international trade.   Thus, trade between any two countries is negatively correlated with geographical distance (ln D) between them whereas the existence of common borders (BORDER) tends to increase the extent of such trade.   High trade barriers (ATO) [2] represent another impediment to bilateral trade.

It is further apparent that economic integration contributes to trade

---

[1]   The first two hypotheses pertain to demand factors and the later two to supply factors.   Note further that the inequality measure utilized in the present investigation takes values between 0 and 1, when w refers to the ratio of the particular characteristic in country j to the sum of this characteristic in country j and partner country k.
        INEQ = 1 + [w ln(w) + (1-w) ln (1-w)]/ln 2

[2]   In the absence of data on the height of trade barriers in a number of countries, deviations between actual and hypothetical per capita exports have been used as a proxy for trade orientation, with hypothetical values having been derived from a regression equation incorporating per capita incomes, population, the rate of mineral exports to GNP, and distance from foreign markets as explanatory variables.   (For a detailed explanation and the estimating equation actually employed, see Chapter 2).

among the participating countries. This conclusion applies equally well
to the European Common Market (EEC), the European Free Trade Association
(EFTA), and the Latin American Free Trade Association (LAFTA), which have
been considered in the present investigation.

Similar results have been obtained in regard to language and cultural
groups. Thus, members of these groups tend to trade more with each other
than with non-members. This is shown by the positive signs of the
regression coefficients for the English, French, German, Scandinavian,
Spanish, and Portuguese language and cultural groups.

9.7 Empirical Results for Individual Groups of Countries

Developed countries are not members of LAFTA; they do not belong to the
Spanish and Portuguese language groups; and offshore assembly has little
relevance for trade among them. Correspondingly, these variables have
been eliminated from the estimating equation for trade among the developed
countries. All the remaining gravitational variables are highly
significant statistically, except for the French dummy variable, which is
significant at the 10 percent level.

The results obtained for the developed country group confirm the
hypotheses concerning inter-industry and intra-industry specialization,
the exception being the human capital variable. In the latter case, a
negative rather than a positive sign is obtained, possibly reflecting the
statistical noise associated with the fact that differences among
developed countries in terms of human capital endowments are small.

In the period of investigation, EEC and EFTA did not have developing
country members, the exception being Portugal in the case of EFTA. Nor do
any developing countries belong to the German or Scandinavian language and
cultural groups. Correspondingly, these variables have been omitted in
making estimates for trade among developing countries. The offshore
assembly variable has also been excluded as it has little relevance to
trade among these countries.

All the remaining variables other than that representing border trade are highly significant statistically, and confirm the relevant hypotheses in the estimates for trade among developing countries, the only exception being the per capita income inequality variable. [1/] In the case of border trade, the intercorrelation between participation in LAFTA and the existence of common borders may have influenced the results.

For reasons adduced in regard to developed and to developing countries, in the estimating equation for trade between the two groups of countries, the EEC, LAFTA, as well as the German, Scandinavian, Spanish, and Portuguese language and cultural group variables have been eliminated. The remaining variables are again highly significant statistically; they confirm the suggested hypotheses in every case.

With one exception, all the variables have the expected sign and are highly significant statistically in the equation estimated for trade among European countries. The exception is the French language variable that is far below even the 10 percent level of significance.

9.8 Summary

This chapter has examined the determinants of international trade in manufactured goods in 152 industries among 38 major exporters of manufactured goods. It has considered the impact on bilateral trade in individual industries of the factors affecting inter-industry and intra-industry specialization, together with that of gravitational factors.

The empirical results obtained for trade among the entire group of countries support the hypotheses put forward in the paper. To begin with, it is apparent that the relative capital intensity of exports is positively correlated with relative capital abundance. This conclusion applies equally well to physical and to human capital.

[1/] It should be noted that the proportion of unobserved tradeflows in 86% in trade among developing countries. The very high degree of censoring may be the cause of this unexpected result.

While factors determining comparative advantage explain inter-industry specialization, or net trade, a variety of factors contribute to intra-industry specialization, or mutual trade among pairs of countries. The results show that trade between any two countries is positively correlated with their average per capita income and country size and negatively correlated with intercountry differences in these variables. Also, product differentiation tends to increase and product standardization reduce intra-industry, and hence total, trade. Finally, offshore assembly has a positive impact on intra-industry trade.

Among gravitational factors, distance is a barrier to trade whereas the existence of common borders has the opposite effect. High trade barriers also hinder bilateral trade. Finally, participation in integration schemes as well as common language and culture tend to promote trade among the countries concerned.

The geographical disaggregation of the estimates indicates the robustness of the results. Thus, the estimates for trade among developed countries, among developing countries, and between developed and developing countries support the stated hypotheses, the only exception being the human capital intensity of trade in the first case and per capita income inequality in the second.

This chapter has successfully tested hypotheses pertaining to intra-industry and inter-industry trade, as well as the effects of gravitational factors, in the framework of a multi-country and multi-industry model. The results may be interpreted to indicate changes in the pattern of inter-industry and intra-industry specialization in the process of economic development.

REFERENCES

1 Amemiya, T., A note on a random coefficients model, International Economic Review 19:3 (1978) 793-796.

2 Aquino, A., Intra-industry trade and inter-industry specialization as concurrent sources of international trade in manufactures, Weltwirtschaftliches Archiv 114:2 (1978) 275-296.

3 Aw, B.-Y., The interpretation of cross-section regression tests of the Heckscher-Ohlin theorem with many goods and factors, Journal of International Economics 14:1/2 (1983) 163-167.

4 Balassa, B., Trade liberalization and 'revealed' comparative advantage, Manchester School 33:2 (1965) 99-123.

5 Balassa, B., Tariff reductions and trade in manufactures among the industrial countries, American Economic Review 56:3 (1966) 466-473.

6 Balassa, B., Trade Liberalization among Industrial Countries: Objectives and Alternatives (McGraw Hill, New York, for the Council on Foreign Relations, 1967), Chapter 5.

7 Balassa, B., European Economic Integration (North-Holland, Amsterdam, 1975), Chapter 2.

8 Balassa, B., Effects of commercial policy on international trade, the location of production, and factor movements, in: Ohlin, B., Hesselborn P., and Wijkman, P. M. (eds.), The International Allocation of Economic Activity (Macmillan, London, 1977).

9   Balassa, B., Intra-industry trade and the integration of developing countries in the world economy, in: Giersch, H. (ed.), On the Economics of Intra-Industry Trade (J.C.B. Mohr, Tubingen, 1979).

10 Balassa, B., The changing pattern of comparative advantage in manufactured goods, Review of Economics and Statistics 56:2 (1979) 259-266. Cited as Balassa, 1979a.

11 Balassa, B., A 'stages approach' to comparative advantage, in: Adelman, I. (ed.), Economic Growth and Resources, Volume 4: National and International Issues (Macmillan, London, 1979). Republished as Essay 6 in B. Balassa, The Newly Industrializing Countries in the World Economy (Pergamon Press, New York, 1981).

12 Balassa, B., Structural adjustment policies in developing countries, World Development 10:1 (1983) 23-38.

13 Balassa, B., Exports, policy choices and economic growth in developing countries after the 1973 oil shock, Journal of Development Economics 18:1 (1985) 23-36.

14 Balassa, B., Comparative advantage in manufactured goods: a re-appraisal, Review of Economics and Statistics 68:2 (1986) 315-319.

15 Balassa, B., Stages approach to comparative advantage revisited, Prévision et Analyse Economique 5:1 (1984) pp. 29-54.

16 Baldwin, R. E., Determinants of the commodity structure of U.S. trade, American Economic Review 53:1 (1971) 126-146.

17 Baldwin, R. E., Determinants of trade and foreign investment: further evidence, Review of Economics and Statistics 61:1 (1979) 40-48.

18 Bergstrand, J.H., Measurement and determinants of intra-industry international trade, in: Tharakan, P.K.M. (ed.) Intra-Industry Trade (North-Holland, Amsterdam, 1983).

19 Bowden, R., An Empirical Model of Bilateral Trade (or Its Absence) in
Manufactured Commodities, paper presented at the Australasian Conference
of the Econometric Society (1983).

20 Bowen, H. P., Changes in the international distribution of resources and
their impact on U.S. comparative advantage, Review of Economics and
Statistics 65:3 (1983) 402-414.

21 Brander, J. A., Intra-industry trade in identical commodities, Journal of
International Economics 11:1 (1981) 1-14.

22 Branson, W. H., Factor Inputs, U.S. Trade and the Heckscher-Ohlin Model,
Seminar Paper No. 27, Institute for International Economic Studies,
University of Stockholm (1973).

23 Branson, W. H. and Monoyios, N., Factor inputs in U.S. trade, Journal of
International Economics 7:2 (1977) 111-131.

24 Caves, R. E., Intra-industry trade and market structure in the industrial
countries, Oxford Economic Papers 33:2 (1981) 203-223.

25 Caves, R. E., Porter, M. E., and Spence, A. M., with Scott, J. T.,
Competition in the Open Economy: A Model Applied to Canada (Harvard
University Press, Cambridge, Mass., 1980).

26 Chenery, H. B., Patterns of industrial growth, American Economic Review
50:4 (1960) 624-654.

27 Clair, C., Gaussens, O., and Phan,D.-L., Le commerce international intra-
branche et ses déterminants d'après le schéma de concurrence
monopolistique: une vérification empirique, Revue Economique 35:2 (1984)
347-378.

28 Deardorff, A. V., The general validity of the Heckscher-Ohlin theorem,
American Economic Review 72:4 (1982) 683-694.

29 Dixit, A. K. and Norman, V., Theory of International Trade (James Nisbet
& Co. and Cambridge University Press, Digswell Place, Welwyn, 1980).

30 Drèze, J., Quelques réflexions sereines sur l'adaptation de l'industrie
    belge au Marché commun, Comptes rendus des Travaux de la Sociétè Royale
    d'Economie Politique de Belgique No. 275 (1980).

31 Eastman, H. C. and Stykolt, S., The Tariff and Competition in Canada
    (Macmillan, Toronto, 1967).

32 Fallon, P. R., and Layard, P. R. G., Capital-skill complementarity,
    income distribution, and output accounting, Journal of Political Economy
    83:2 (1975) 279-301.

33 Falvey, R. F., Commercial policy and intra-industry trade, Journal of
    International Economics 11:4 (1981) 495-511.

34 Fels, G., The choice of industry mix in the division of labour between
    developed and developing countries, Weltwirtschaftliches Archiv 108:1
    (1972) 71-121.

35 Gray, H. P. and Martin, J. P., The meaning and measurement of product
    differentiation in international trade, Weltwirtschaftliches Archiv 116:2
    (1980) 322-319.

36 Greenaway, D. and Milner, C., Trade imbalance effects and the measurement
    of intra-industry trade, Welwirtschaftliches Archiv 117:4 (1981) 756-762.

37 Grubel, H. G. and Lloyd, P. J., Intra-Industry Trade (Macmillan, London,
    1975).

38 Gruber, W. H. and Vernon, R., The technology factor in a world trade
    matrix, in: Vernon, R. (ed.) The Technology Factor in International
    Trade (National Bureau of Economic Research, Columbia University Press,
    New York, 1970).

39 Harbison, F. H., Maruhnic, J. and Resnick, J. R., Quantitative Analyses
    of Modernization and Development (Industrial Relations Section, Dept. of
    Economics, Princeton University, Princeton, 1970).

40 Havrylyshyn, O. and Civan, E., Intra-industry trade and the stage of development: a regression analysis of industrial and developing countries, in: Tharakan, P. K. M. (ed.) Intra-Industry Trade (North-Holland, Amsterdam, 1983)

41 Helpman, E., International trade in the presence of product differentiation, economies of scale and monopolistic competition: a Chamberlin-Heckscher-Ohlin approach, Journal of International Economics 11:3 (1981) 305-340.

42 Helpman, E. and Krugman, P., Market Structure and Foreign Trade: Increasing Returns, Imperfect Competition, and the International Economy (MIT Press, Cambridge, Mass., 1986).

43 Hirsch, S., The product cycle model of international trade - A multi-country cross section analysis, Oxford Bulletin of Economics and Statistics 37:4 (1975) 305-317.

44 Hufbauer, G. C., The impact of national characteristics and technology on the commodity composition of trade in manufactured goods, in: Vernon, R. (ed.) The Technology Factor in International Trade (National Bureau of Economic Research, New York, 1970).

45 Johnson, H. G., The state of theory in relation to empirical analysis, in: The Technology Factor in International Trade, op.cit.

46 Kenan, P. B., Nature, capital, and trade, Journal of Political Economy 73:5 (1965) 437-460.

47 Krueger, A. O., Trade and Employment in Developing Countries, Vol. 3, Synthesis and Conclusions (The University of Chicago Press, Chicago, 1987).

48 Krugman, P. R., Scale economies, product differentiation, and the pattern of trade, American Economic Review 70:5 (1980) 950-959.

49 Lancaster, K., Intra-industry trade under perfect monopolistic competition, Journal of International Economics 10:2 (1980) 151-175.

50 Lary, H. B., Imports of Manufactures from Less-Developed Countries, (National Bureau of Economic Research, Columbia University Press, New York, 1968).

51 Lary, H. B., Comments on the technology factor in a world trade matrix, in: The Technology Factor in International Trade, op.cit.

52 Leamer, E. E., The commodity composition of international trade in manufactures: an empirical analysis, Oxford Economic Papers 26:3 (1974) 350-374.

53 Leamer, E. E., Sources of International Comparative Advantage: Theory and Evidence (MIT Press, Cambridge, Mass., 1981).

54 Linder, S. B., An Essay on Trade and Transformation (John Wiley, New York, 1961).

55 Loertscher, R. and Wolter, F., Determinants of intra-industry trade: among countries and across industries, Weltwirtschaftliches Archiv 116(2) (1980) 280-292.

56 Lundberg, L., Intra-industry trade: the case of Sweden, Weltwirtschaftliches Archiv 118(2) (1982) 303-316.

57 Maddala, G. S., Limited-Dependent and Qualitative Variables in Econometrics (Cambridge University Press, Cambridge, 1983).

58 Maskus, K. E., Evidence on shifts in the determinants of the structure of U.S. manufacturing foreign trade, 1958-76, Review of Economics and Statistics 65:3 (1983) 415-422.

59 McDonald, J.F. and Moffit, R. A., The uses of tobit analysis, Review of Economics and Statistics 62:2 (1980) 318-321.

60 Noland, M., Econometric Estimation of International Intraindustry Trade, Institute for International Economics, Washington, D.C. (August 1987).

61 Noland, M., The determinants of international specialization in manufactured goods, 1965-1980, Economic Studies Quarterly (1988) forthcoming.

62 Pagoulatos, E. and Sorensen, R., Two-way international trade: an econometric analysis, Weltwirtschaftliches Archiv 111(3) (1975) 454-465.

63 Stern, R. M., Some evidence on the factor content of West Germany's foreign trade, Journal of Political Economy 84:1 (1976) 131-141.

64 Stern, R. M., and Maskus, K. E., Determinants of the structure of U. S. foreign trade, 1958-76, Journal of International Economics 11:2 (1981) 207-224.

65 Toh, K. A., Cross-section analysis of intra-industry trade in U.S. manufacturing industries, Weltwirtschaftliches Archiv 118(2) (1982) 282-301.

66 Urata, S., Factor inputs and Japanese manufacturing trade structure, Review of Economics and Statistics 65:4 (1983) 678-684.

67 White, H., A heteroskedasticity-consistent covariance matrix estimator and a direct test for heteroskedasticity, Econometrica 48:4 (1980) 817-838.

INDEX